Stoic Six Pack 8

Stoic Six Pack 8: The Peripatetics

By

George Grote

Alexander Grant

Elbert Hubbard

William De Witt Hyde

Diogenes Laërtius

George Malcolm Stratton

Enhanced Media
2016

Stoic Six Pack 8 - The Peripatetics

Introduction by Elbert Hubbard. From *Little Journeys to the Homes of Great Philosophers - Aristotle* by Elbert Hubbard. First published in 1916.

Lyco of Troas by Diogenes Laërtius. From *The Lives and Opinions of Eminent Philosophers* by Diogenes Laërtius, translated by Charles Duke Yonge. First published in 1853.

The Aristotelian Sense of Proportion by William De Witt Hyde. First published in *The Five Great Philosophies of Life* by William De Witt Hyde, 1911.

Strato of Lampsacus by Diogenes Laërtius. From *The Lives and Opinions of Eminent Philosophers* by Diogenes Laërtius, translated by Charles Duke Yonge. First published in 1853.

Life of Aristotle by George Grote. First published in 1872.

Theophrastus by George Malcolm Stratton. From *Theophrastus and the Greek physiological psychology before Aristotle* by George Malcolm Stratton. First published in 1917.

Post-Aristotelian Philosophy: The Stoics by Alexander Grant. From *The Ethics of Aristotle: Illustrated with Essays and Notes (Volume I)* published in 1885.

Published by Enhanced Media.

Enhanced Media Publishing
Los Angeles, CA.

First Printing: 2016.

ISBN-13: 978-1530349562

ISBN-10: 1530349567

Contents

Introduction by Elbert Hubbard 7
Lyco of Troas by Diogenes Laërtius 20
The Aristotelian Sense of Proportion by William Hyde .. 24
Strato of Lampsacus by Diogenes Laërtius 45
Life of Aristotle by George Grote 48
Theophrastus by George Malcolm Stratton 64
Post-Aristotelian Philosophy: The Stoics by Alexander Grant 81

Introduction by Elbert Hubbard

Happiness itself is sufficient excuse. Beautiful things are right and true; so beautiful actions are those pleasing to the gods. Wise men have an inward sense of what is beautiful, and the highest wisdom is to trust this intuition and be guided by it. The answer to the last appeal of what is right lies within a man's own breast. Trust thyself.

— Ethics of Aristotle.

Aristotle was born Three Hundred Eighty-four B.C., at the village of Stagira in the mountains of Macedonia. King Amyntas used to live at Stagira several months in the year and hunt the wild hogs that fed on the acorns which grew in the gorges and valleys. Mountain climbing and hunting was dangerous sport, and it was well to have a surgeon attached to the royal party, so the father of Aristotle served in that capacity. No doubt, though, but the whole outfit was decidedly barbaric, even including the doctor's little son "Aristo," who refused to be left behind. The child's mother had died years before, and boys without mothers are apt to manage their fathers. And so Aristo was allowed to trot along by his father's side, carrying a formidable bow, which he himself had made, with a quiver of arrows at his back.

Those were great times when the King came to Stagira!

When the King went back to the capital everybody received presents, and the good doctor, by some chance, was treated best of all, and little Aristo came in for the finest bow that ever was, all tipped with silver and eagle-feathers. But the bow did not bring good luck, for soon after, the boy's father was caught in an avalanche of sliding stone and crushed to death.

Aristo was taken in charge by Proxenus, a near kinsman. The lad was so active at climbing, so full of life and energy and good spirits, that when the King came the next year to Stagira, he asked for Aristo. With the King was his son Philip, a lad about the age of Aristo, but not so tall nor so active. The boys became fast friends, and once when a stranger saw them together he complimented the King on his fine, intelligent boys, and the King had to explain, "The other boy is mine—but I wish they both were."

Aristo knew where the wild boars fed in gulches, and where the stunted oaks grew close and thick. Higher up in the mountains there were bears, which occasionally came down and made the wild pigs scamper. You could always tell when the bears were around, for then the little pigs would run out into the open. The bears had a liking for little pigs, and the bears had a liking for the honey in the bee-trees, too. Aristo could find the bee-trees better than the bears—all you had to do was to watch the flight of the bees as they left the clover.

Then there were deer—you could see their tracks any time around the mountain marshes where the springs gushed forth and the watercress grew lush. Still higher up the mountains, beyond where bears ever traveled, there were mountain-sheep, and still higher up were goats. The goats were so wild that hardly any one but Aristo had ever seen them, but he knew they were there.

The King was delighted to have such a lad as companion for his son, and insisted that he should go back to the capital with them and become a member of the Court.

Not he—there were other ambitions. He wanted to go to Athens and study at the school of Plato—Plato, the pupil of the great Socrates.

The King laughed—he had never heard of Plato. That a youth should refuse to become part of the Macedonian Court, preferring the company of an unknown school-master, was amusing—he laughed.

The next year when the King came back to Stagira, Aristo was still there. "And you haven't gone to Athens yet?" said the King.

"No, but I am going," was the firm reply.

"We will send him," said the King to Proxenus, Aristo's guardian.

And so we find Aristo, aged seventeen, tall and straight and bronzed, starting off for Athens, his worldly goods rolled up in a bearskin, tied about with thongs. There is a legend to the effect that Philip went with Aristo, and that for a time they were together at Plato's school. But, anyway, Philip did not remain long. Aristo—or Aristotle, we had better call him—remained with Plato just twenty years.

At Plato's school Aristotle was called by the boys, "the Stagirite," a name that was to last him through life—and longer. In Winter he wore his bearskin, caught over one shoulder, for a robe, and his mountain grace and native beauty of mind and body must have been a joy to Plato from the first. Such a youth could not be overlooked.

To him that hath shall be given. The pupil that wants to learn is the teacher's favorite—which is just as it should not be. Plato proved his humanity by giving his all to the young mountaineer. Plato was then a little over sixty years of age—about the same age that Socrates was when Plato became his pupil. But the years had touched Plato lightly—unlike Socrates, he had endured no Thracian winters in bare feet, neither had he lived on cold snacks picked up here and there, as Providence provided. Plato was a bachelor. He still wore the purple robe, proud, dignified, yet gentle, and his back was straight as that of a youth. Lowell once said, "When I hear Plato's name mentioned, I always think of George William Curtis—a combination of pride and intellect, a man's strength fused with a woman's gentleness."

Plato was an aristocrat. He accepted only such pupils as he invited, or those that were sent by royalty. Like Franz Liszt, he charged no tuition, which plan, by the way, is a good scheme for getting more money than could otherwise be obtained, although no such selfish charge should be brought against either Plato or Liszt. Yet every benefit must be paid for, and whether you use the word fee or honorarium, matters little. I hear there be lecturers who accept invitations to banquets and accept an honorarium mysteriously placed on the mantel, when they would scorn a fee.

Plato's Garden School, where the pupils reclined under the trees on marble benches, and read and talked, or listened to lectures by the Master, was almost an ideal place. Not the ideal for us, because we believe that the mental and the manual must go hand in hand. The world of intellect should not be separated from the world of work. It was too much to expect that in a time when slavery was everywhere, Plato would see the fallacy of having one set of men to do the thinking, and another do the work. We haven't got far from that yet; only free men can see the whole truth, and a free man is one who lives in a country where there are no slaves. To own slaves is to be one, and to live in a land of slavery is to share in the bondage—a partaker in the infamy and the profits.

Plato and Aristotle became fast friends—comrades. With thinking men years do not count—only those grow old who think by proxy. Plato had no sons after the flesh, and the love of his heart went out to the Stagirite: in him he saw his own life projected.

When Aristotle had turned twenty he was acquainted with all the leading thinkers of his time; he read constantly, wrote, studied and conversed. The little property his father left had come to him; the King of Macedon sent him presents; and he taught various pupils from wealthy families—finances were easy. But success did not spoil him. The brightest scholars do not make the greatest success in life, because alma mater usually catches them for teachers. Sometimes this is well, but more often it is not. Plato would not hear of Aristotle's leaving him, and so he remained, the chief ornament and practical leader of the school.

He became rich, owned the largest private library at Athens, and was universally regarded as the most learned man of his time.

In many ways he had surpassed Plato. He delved into natural history, collected plants, rocks, animals, and made studies of the practical workings of economic schemes. He sought to divest the Platonic teaching of its poetry, discarded rhetoric, and tried to get at the simple truth of all subjects.

Toward the last of Plato's career this repudiation by Aristotle of poetry, rhetoric, elocution and the polite accomplishments caused a schism to break out in the Garden School. Plato's head was in the clouds at times; Aristotle's was, too, but his feet were always on the earth.

When Plato died, Aristotle was his natural successor as leader of the school, but there was opposition to him, both on account of his sturdy, independent ways and because he was a foreigner.

He left Athens to become a member of the Court of Hermias, a former pupil, now King of Atarneus.

He remained here long enough to marry the niece of his patron, and doubtless saw himself settled for life—a kingly crown within his reach should his student-sovereign pass away.

And the royal friend did pass away, by the dagger's route. As life-insurance risks I am told that Kings have to pay double premium. Revolution broke out, and as Aristotle was debating in his mind what course to pursue, a messenger with soldiers arrived from King Philip of Macedon, offering safe convoy, enclosing transportation, and asking that Aristotle come and take charge of the education of his son, Alexander, aged thirteen.

Aristotle did not wait to parley: he accepted the invitation. Horses were saddled, camels packed and that night, before the moon arose, the cavalcade silently moved out into the desert.

The offer that had been made twenty-four years before, by Philip's father, was now accepted. Aristotle was forty-two years old, in the prime of his power. Time had tempered his passions, but not subdued his zest in life. He had the curious, receptive, alert and eager mind of a child. His intellect was at its ripest and best. He was a lover of animals, and all outdoor life appealed to him as it does to a growing boy. He was a daring horseman, and we hear of his riding off into the desert and sleeping on the sands, his horse untethered watching over him. Aristotle was the first man to make a scientific study of the horse, and with the help of Alexander he set up a skeleton, fastening the bones in place, to the mighty astonishment of the natives, who mistook the feat for an attempt to make a living animal; and when the beast was not at last saddled and bridled there were subdued chuckles of satisfaction among the "hoi polloi" at the failure of the scheme, and murmurs of "I told you so!"

Eighteen hundred years were to pass before another man was to take up the horse as a serious scientific study; and this was Leonardo da Vinci, a man in many ways very much like Aristotle. The distinguishing feature in these men—the thing that differentiates them from other men—was the great outpouring sympathy with every living creature. Everything they saw was related to themselves—it came very close to them—they wanted to know more about it. This is essentially the child-mind, and the calamity of life is to lose it.

Leonardo became interested in Aristotle's essay on the horse, and continued the subject further, dissecting the animal in minutest detail and illustrating his discoveries with painstaking drawings. His work is so complete and exhaustive that nobody nowadays has time to more than read the title-page. Leonardo's bent was natural science, and his first attempts at drawing were done to illustrate his books. Art was beautiful, of course—it brought in an income, made friends and brought him close to people who saw nothing unless you made a picture of it. He made pictures for recreation and to amuse folks, and his threat to put the peeping Prior into the "Last Supper," posed as Judas, revealed his contempt for the person to whom a picture was just a picture. The marvel to Leonardo was the mind that could imagine, the hand that could execute, and the soul that could see.

And the curious part is that Leonardo lives for us through his play and not through his serious work. His science has been superseded, but his art is immortal.

This expectant mental attitude, this attitude of worship, belongs to all great scientists. The man divines the thing first and then looks for it, just as the Herschels knew where the star ought to be and then patiently waited for it. The Bishop of London said that if Darwin had spent one-half as much time in reading his Bible as in studying earthworms, he would have really benefited the world, and saved his soul alive. To Walt Whitman, a hair on the back of his hand was just as curious and wonderful as the stars in the sky, or God's revelation to man through a printed book.

Aristotle loved animals as a boy loves them—his house was a regular menagerie of pets, and into this world of life Alexander was very early introduced. We hear of young Alexander breaking the wild horse, Bucephalus, and beyond a doubt Aristotle was seated on the top rail of the paddock when he threw the lariat.

Aristotle and his pupil had the first circus of which we know, and they also inaugurated the first Zoological Garden mentioned in history, barring Noah, of course.

So much was Alexander bound up in this menagerie, and in his old teacher as well, that in after-life, in all of his travels, he was continually sending back to Aristotle specimens of every sort of bird, beast and fish to be found in the countries through which he traveled.

When Philip was laid low by the assassin's thrust, it was Aristotle who backed up Alexander, aged twenty—but a man—in his prompt suppression of the revolution. The will that had been used to subdue man-eating stallions and to train wild animals, now came in to repress riot, and the systematic classification of things was a preparation for the forming of an army out of a mob. Aristotle said, "An army is a huge animal with a million claws—it must have only one brain, and that the commander's."

Alexander gave credit again and again to Aristotle for those elements in his character that went to make up success: steadiness of purpose, self-reliance, systematic effort, mathematical calculation, attention to details, and a broad and generous policy that sees the end.

When Aristotle argued with Philip, years before, that horse-breaking should be included in the educational curriculum of all young men, he evidently divined football and was endeavoring to supplant it.

I think history has been a trifle severe on Alexander. He was elected Captain-General of Greece, and ordered to repel the Persian invasion. And he did the business once for all. War is not all fighting—Providence is on the side of the strongest commissariat. Alexander had to train, arm, clothe and feed a million men, and march them long miles across a desert country. The real foe of a man is in his own heart, and the foe of an army is in its own camp—disease takes more prisoners than the enemy. Fever sniped more of our boys in blue than did the hostile Filipinos.

Alexander's losses were principally from men slain in battle; from this, I take it that Alexander knew a deal of sanitary science, and had a knowledge of practical mathematics, in order to systematize that mob of restless, turbulent helots. We hear of Aristotle cautioning him that safety lies in keeping his men busy—they must not have too much time to think, otherwise mutiny is to be feared. Still, they must not be over-worked, or they will be in no condition to fight when the eventful time occurs. And we are amazed to see this: "Do not let your men drink out of stagnant pools—Athenians, city-born, know no better. And when you carry water on the desert marches, it should be first boiled to prevent its getting sour."

Concerning the Jews, Alexander writes to his teacher and says, 'They are apt to be in sullen rebellion against their governors, receiving orders only from their high priests, and this leads to severe measures, which are construed as persecution"; all of which might have been written yesterday by the Czar in a message to The Hague Convention.

Alexander captured the East, and was taken captive by the East Like the male bee that never lives to tell the tale of its wooing, he succeeded and died. Yet he vitalized all Asia with the seeds of Greek philosophy, turned back the hungry barbaric tide, and made a new map of the Eastern world. He built far more cities than he destroyed. He set Andrew Carnegie an example at Alexandria, such as the world had never up to that time seen. At the entrance to the harbor of the same city he erected a lighthouse, surpassing far the one at Minot's Ledge, or Race Rock. This structure endured for two centuries, and when at last wind and weather had their way, there was no Hopkinson Smith who could erect another.

At Thebes, Alexander paid a compliment to letters, by destroying every building in the city except the house of the poet, Pindar. At Corinth, when the great, the wise, the noble, came to pay homage, one great man did not appear. In vain did Alexander look for his card among all those handed in at the door—Diogenes, the Philosopher, oft quoted by Aristotle, was not to be seen.

Alexander went out to hunt him up, and found him sunning himself, propped up against the wall in the Public Square, busy doing nothing.

The philosopher did not arise to greet the conqueror; he did not even offer a nod of recognition.

"I am Alexander—is there not something I can do for you?" modestly asked the descendant of Hercules.

"Just stand out from between me and the sun," replied the philosopher, and went on with his meditations.

Alexander enjoyed the reply so much that he said to his companions, and afterward wrote to Aristotle, "If I were not Alexander, I would be Diogenes," and thus did strenuosity pay its tribute to self-sufficiency.

Aristotle might have assumed important affairs of State, but practical politics were not to his liking. "What Aristotle is in the world of thought I will be in the world of action," said Alexander.

On all of his journeys Alexander found time to keep in touch with his old teacher at home; and we find the ruler of Asia voicing that old request, "Send me something to read," and again, "I live alone with my thoughts, amidst a throng of men, but without companions."

Plutarch gives a copy of a letter sent by Alexander wherein Aristotle is chided for publishing his lecture on oratory. "Now all the world will know what formerly belonged to you and me alone," plaintively cries the young man who sighed for more worlds to conquer, and therein shows he was the victim of a fallacy that will never die—the idea that truth can be embodied in a book. When will we ever learn that inspired books demand inspired readers!

There are no secrets. A book may stimulate thought, but it can never impart it.

Aristotle wrote out the Laws of Oratory. "Alas!" groans Alexander, "everybody will turn orator now." But he was wrong, because Oratory and the Laws of Oratory are totally different things.

A Boston man of excellent parts has just recently given out the Sixteen Perfective Laws of Oratory, and the Nineteen Steps in Evolution.

The real truth is, there are Fifty-seven Varieties of Artistic Vagaries, and all are valuable to the man who evolves them—they serve him as a scaffolding whereby he builds thought. But woe betide Alexander and all rare-ripe Bostonians who mistake the scaffolding for the edifice.

There are no Laws of Art. A man evolves first, and builds his laws afterward. The style is the man, and a great man, full of the spirit, will express himself in his own way.

Bach ignored all the Laws of Harmony made before his day and set down new ones—and these marked his limitations, that was all. Beethoven upset all these, and Wagner succeeded by breaking most of Beethoven's rules. And now comes Grieg, and writes harmonious discords that Wagner said were impossible, and still it is music, for by it we are transported on the wings of song and uplifted to the stars.

The individual soul striving for expression ignores all man-made laws. Truth is that which serves us best in expressing our lives. A rotting log is truth to a bed of violets, while sand is truth to a cactus. But when the violet writes a book on "Expression as I Have Found It," making laws for the evolution of beautiful blossoms, it leaves the Century Plant out of its equation, or else swears, i' faith, that a cactus is not a flower, and that a Night-Blooming Cereus is a disordered thought from a madman's brain. And when the proud and lofty cactus writes a book it never mentions violets, because it has never stooped to seek them.

Art is the blossoming of the Soul.

We can not make the plant blossom—all we can do is to comply with the conditions of growth. We can supply the sunshine, moisture and aliment, and God does the rest. In teaching, he only is successful who supplies the conditions of growth—that is all there is of the Science of Pedagogics, which is not a science, and if it ever becomes one, it will be the Science of Letting Alone, and not a scheme of interference. Just so long as some of the greatest men are those who have broken through pedagogic fancy and escaped, succeeding by breaking every rule of pedagogy, as Wagner discarded every Law of Harmony, there will be no such thing as a Science of Education.

Recently I read Aristotle's Essays on Rhetoric and Oratory, and I was pained to see how I had been plagiarized by this man who wrote three hundred years before Christ. Aristotle used charts in teaching and indicated the mean by a straight horizontal line, and the extreme by an upright dash. He says: "From one extreme the mean looks extreme, and from another extreme the mean looks small—it all depends upon your point of view. Beware of jumping to conclusions, for beside the appearance you must look within and see from what vantage-ground you gain the conclusions. All truth is relative, and none can be final to a man six feet high, who stands on the ground, who can walk but forty miles at a stretch, who needs four meals a day and one-third of his time for sleep. A loss of sleep, or loss of a meal, or a meal too much, will disarrange his point of view, and change his opinions." And thus do we see that a belief in "eternal punishment" is a mere matter of indigestion.

A certain bishop, we have seen, experienced a regret that Darwin expended so much time on earthworms; and we might also express regret that Aristotle did not spend more. As long as he confined himself to earth, he was eminently sure and right: he was really the first man who ever used his eyes. But when he quit the earth, and began to speculate about the condition of souls before they are clothed with bodies, or what becomes of them after they discard the body, or the nature of God, he shows that he knew no more than we. That is to say, he knew no more than the barbarians who preceded him.

He attempted to grasp ideas which Herbert Spencer pigeonholes forever as the Unknowable; and in some of his endeavors to make plain the unknowable, Aristotle strains language to the breaking-point—the net bursts and all of his fish go free. Here is an Aristotelian proposition, expressed by Hegel to make lucid a thing nobody comprehends: "Essential being as being that meditates with itself, with itself by the negativity of itself, is relative to itself only as it is relative to another; that is, immediate only as something posited and meditated." It gives one a slight shock to hear him speak of headache being caused by wind on the brain, or powdered grasshopper-wings being a cure for gout, but when he calls the heart a pump that forces the blood to the extremities, we see that he anticipates Harvey, although more than two thousand years of night lie between them.

Some of Aristotle reads about like this Geometrical Domestic Equation:
Definitions:

All boarding-houses are the same boarding-houses.

Boarders in the same boarding-house, and on the same flat, are equal to one another.

A single room is that which hath no parts and no magnitude.

The landlady of the boarding-house is a parallelogram—that is, an oblong figure that can not be described, and is equal to anything.

A wrangle is the disinclination to each other of two boarders that meet together, but are not on the same floor.

All the other rooms being taken, a single room is a double room.

Postulates and Propositions:

A pie may be produced any number of times.

The landlady may be reduced to her lowest terms by a series of propositions.

A bee-line is the shortest distance between the Phalanstery and By Allen's.

The clothes of a boarding-house bed stretched both ways will not meet.

Any two meals at a boarding-house are together less than one meal at the Phalanstery.

On the same bill and on the same side of it there should not be two charges for the same thing.

If there be two boarders on the same floor, and the amount of the side of the one be equal to the amount of the side of the other, and the wrangle between the one boarder and the landlady be equal to the wrangle between the landlady and the other boarder, then shall the weekly bills of the two boarders be equal. For, if not, let one bill be the greater, then the other bill is less than it might have been, which is absurd. Therefore the bills are equal.

Quod erat demonstrandum.

The business of the old philosophers was to philosophize. To philosophize as a business is to miss the highest philosophy. To do a certain amount of useful work every day, and not trouble about either the past or the future, is the highest wisdom. The man who drags the past behind him, and dives into the future, spreads the present out thin. Therein lies the bane of most religions. A man goes out into the woods to study the birds: he walks and walks and walks and sees no birds. But just let him sit down on a log and wait, and lo! the branches are full of song.

Those who pursue Culture never catch up with her. Culture takes alarm at pursuit and avoids the stealthy pounce. Culture is a woman, and a certain amount of indifference wins her. Ardent wooing will not secure either wisdom or a woman—except in the case where a woman marries a man to get rid of him, and then he really does not get the woman—he only secures her husk. And the husks of culture are pedantry and sciolism. The highest philosophy of the future will consist in doing each day that which is most useful. Talking about it will be quite incidental and secondary.

After Alexander had completed his little task of conquering the world, it was his intention to sit down and improve his mind. He was going back to Greece to complete the work Pericles had so well begun. To this end Aristotle had left Macedonia and established his Peripatetic School at Athens. Plato was exclusive, and taught in the Garden with its high walls. Aristotle taught in the "peripatos," or porch of the Lyceum, and his classes were for all who wished to attend. Socrates was really the first peripatetic philosopher, but he was a roustabout. Nothing sanctifies like death—and now

Socrates had become respectable, and his methods were to be made legal and legitimate.

Socrates discovered the principle of human liberty; he taught the rights of the individual, and as these threatened to interfere with the State, the politicians got alarmed and put him to death. Plato, much more cautious, wrote his "Republic," wherein everything is subordinated for the good of the State, and the individual is but a cog in a most perfectly lubricated machine. Aristotle saw that Socrates was nearer right than Plato—sin is the expression of individuality and is not wholly bad—the State is made up of individuals, and if you suppress the thinking-power of the individual, you will get a weak and effeminate body politic; there will be none to govern. The whole fabric will break down of its own weight. A man must have the privilege of making a fool of himself—within proper bounds, of course. To that end learning must be for all, and liberty both to listen and to teach should be the privilege of every man.

This is a problem that Boston has before it today: Shall free speech be allowed on the Common? William Morris tried it in Trafalgar Square, to his sorrow; but in Hyde Park, if you think you have a message, London will let you give it. But this is not considered good form, and the "Best Society" listen to no speeches in the park. However, there are signs that Aristotle's outdoor school may come back. Phillips Brooks tried outdoor preaching, and if his health had not failed, he might have popularized it. It only wants a man who is big enough to inaugurate it.

Aristotle had various helpers, and arranged to give his lectures and conferences daily in certain porches or promenades. These lectures covered the whole range of human thought—logic, rhetoric, oratory, physics, ethics, politics, esthetics, and physical culture. These outdoor talks were called exoteric, and there gradually grew up esoteric lessons, which were for the rich or luxurious and the dainty. And there being money in the esoteric lessons, these gradually took the place of the exoteric, and so we get the genesis of our modern private school or college, where we send our children to be taught great things by great men, for a consideration.

Will the exoteric, peripatetic school come back?

I think so.

I believe that university education will soon be free to every boy and girl in America, and this without going far from home. Esoteric education is always more or less of a sham. Our public-school system is purely exoteric, only we stop too soon. We also give our teachers too much work and too little pay. Stop building warships, and use the money to double the teachers' salaries, making the profession respectable, raise the standard of efficiency, and the free university with the old Greek Lyceum will be here.

America must do this—the Old World can't. We have the money, and we have the men and the women; all that is needed is the desire, and this is fast awakening.

When Alexander died, of acute success, aged thirty-two, Aristotle's sustaining prop was gone. The Athenians never thought much of the Macedonians—not much more than Saint Paul did, he having tried to convert both and failed.

Athens was jealous of the power of Alexander: that a provincial should thus rule the Mother-Country was unforgivable. It was as if a Canadian should make himself King of England!

Everybody knew that Aristotle had been the tutor of Alexander, and that they were close friends. And that a Macedonian should be the chief school-teacher in Athens was an affront. The very greatness of the man was his offense: Athens had none to match him, and the world has never since matched him, either. How to get rid of the Macedonian philosopher was the question.

And so our old friend, heresy, comes in again. A poem was found, written by Aristotle many years before, on the death of his friend, King Hermias, wherein Apollo was disrespectfully mentioned. It was the old charge against Socrates come back—the hemlock was brewing. But life was sweet to Aristotle; he chose discretion to valor, and fled to his country home at Chalcis in Euboea.

The humiliation of being driven from his work, and the sudden change from active life to exile, undermined his strength, and he died in a year, aged sixty-two.

In morals the world has added nothing new to the philosophy of Aristotle: gentleness, consideration, moderation, mutual helpfulness, and the principle that one man's privileges end where another man's rights begin— these make up the sum. And on them, all authorities agree, and have for twenty-five hundred years.

The family relations of Aristotle were most exemplary. The unseemly wrangles of Philip and his wife were never repeated in the home of Aristotle. Yet we will have to offer this fact in the interests of stirpiculture: the inconstant Philip and the termagant Olympias brought into the world Alexander; whereas the sons of Aristotle lived their day and died, without making a ripple on the surface of history.

As in the scientific study of the horse, no progress was made from the time of Aristotle to that of Leonardo, so Hegel says there was no advancement in philosophy from the time of Aristotle to that of Spinoza.

Eusebius called Aristotle "Nature's Private Secretary."

Dante spoke of him as the "Master of those who know."

Sir William Hamilton said, "In the range of his powers and perceptions, only Leonardo can be compared with him."

Lyco of Troas by Diogenes Laërtius

He [Strato] was succeeded [as head of the Peripatetic School] by Lyco, a native of the Troas, the son of Astyanax, a man of great eloquence, and of especial ability in the education of youth. For he used to say that it was fit for boys to be harnessed with modesty and rivalry, as much as for horses to be equipped with a spur and a bridle. And his eloquence and energy in speaking is apparent, from this instance. For he speaks of a virgin who was poor in the following manner: "A damsel, who, for want of a dowry, goes beyond the seasonable age, is a heavy burden to her father."

They say that Antigonus said with reference to him, that the sweetness and beauty of an apple could not be transferred to anything else, but that one might see, in the case of this man, all these excellencies, in as great perfection as on a tree; and he said this, because he was a surpassingly sweet speaker. On which account, some people prefixed a F to his name. But as a writer, he was very unequal to his reputation. And he used to jest in a careless way, upon those who repented that they had not learnt when they had the opportunity, and who now wished that they had done so, saying, said that they were accusing themselves, showing by a prayer which could not possibly be accomplished, their misplaced repentance for their idleness. He used also to say, that those who deliberated without coming to a right conclusion, erred in their calculations, like men who investigate a correct nature by an incorrect standard, or who look at a face in disturbed water, or a distorted mirror.

Another of his saying was, that many men go in pursuit of the crown to be won in the forum, but few or none seek to attain the one to be gained at the Olympic games.

And as he in many instances gave much advice to the Athenians, he was of exceedingly great service to them.

He was also a person of great neatness in his dress, wearing garments of an unsurpassable delicacy, as we are told by Hermippus. He was at the same time exceedingly devoted to the exercises of the Gymnasium, and a man who was always in excellent condition as to his body, displaying every quality of an athlete (though Antigonus of Carystus, pretends that he was bruised about the ears and dirty); and in his own country he is said to have wrestled and played ball in his birthplace of Ilium.

IV

And he was exceedingly beloved by Eumenes and Attalus, who made him great presents; and Antigonus also tried to seduce him to his court, but was disappointed. And he was so great an enemy to Hieronymus the Peripatetic, that he was the only person 'who would not go to see him on the anniversary festival which he used to celebrate, and which we have mentioned in our life of Arcesilaus.

And he presided over his school forty-four years, as Strato had left it to him in his will, in the hundred and twenty-seventh Olympiad.

He was also a pupil of Panthoides, the dialectician.

He died when he was seventy-four years of age, having been a great sufferer with the gout, and there is an epigram of ours upon him:

Nor shall wise Lycon be forgotten, who
Died of the gout, and much I wonder at it.
For he who ne'er before could walk alone,
Went the long road to hell in a single night.

There were several people of the name of Lycon. The first was a Pythagorean; the second was this man of whom we are speaking; the third was an epic poet; the fourth was an epigrammatic poet.

I have fallen in love with the following will of this philosopher:

"I make the following disposition of my property; if I am unable to withstand this disease: All the property in my house I leave to my brothers Astyanax and Lycon; and I think that they ought to pay all that I owe at Athens, and that I may have borrowed from any one, and also all the expenses that may be incurred for my funeral, and for other customary solemnities. And all that I have in in the city, or in Aegina, I give to Lycon because he bears the same name that I do, and because he has spent the greater part of his life with me, showing me the greatest affection, as it was fitting that he should do, since he was in the place of a son to me.

And I leave my garden walk to those of my friends who like to use it; to Bulo, and Callinus, and Ariston, and Amplicon, and Lycon, and Python, and Aristomachus, and Heracleus, and Lycomedes, and Lycon my nephew. And I desire that they will elect as president him whom they think most likely to remain attached to the pursuit of philosophy, and most capable of holding the school together. And I entreat the rest of my friends to acquiesce in their election, for my sake and that of the place. And I desire that Bulo, and Callinus, and the rest of my friends will manage my funeral and the burning of my body, so that my obsequies may not be either mean or extravagant. And the property which I have in Aegina shall be divided by Lycon after my decease among the young men there, for the purpose of anointing themselves, in order that the memory of me and of him who honoured me, and who showed his affection by useful presents, may be long preserved. And let him erect a statue of me; and as for the place for it, I desire that Diophantus and Heraclides the son of Demetrius, shall select that, and take care that it be suitable for the proposed erection. With the property that I have in the city let Lycon pay all the people of whom I have borrowed any thing since his departure; and let Bulo and Callinus join him in this, and also in discharging all the expenses incurred for my funeral, and for all other customary solemnities, and let him deduct the amount from the funds which I have left in my house, and bequeathed to them both in common. Let him also pay the physicians, Pasithemis and Medias, men who, for their attention to me and for their skill, are very deserving of still greater honour. And I give to the son of Callinus my pair of Thericlean cups; and to his wife I give my pair of Rhodian cups, and my smooth carpet, and my double carpet, and my curtains, and the two best pillows of all that I leave behind me; so that as far as the compliment goes, I may be seen not to have forgotten them. And with respect to those who have been my servants, I make the following disposition:

To Demetrius who has long been freed, I remit the price of his freedom, and I further give five minas, and a cloak, and a tunic, that as he has a great deal of trouble about me, he may pass the rest of his life comfortably. To Criton, the Chalcedonian, I also remit the price of his freedom, and I further give him four minae. Micras I hereby present with his freedom; and I desire Lycon to maintain him, and instruct him for six years from the present time. I also give his freedom to Chares, and desire Lycon to maintain him. And I further give him two minae, and all my books that are published; but those which are not published, I give to Callinus, that he may publish them with due care. I also give to Syrus, whom I have already emancipated, four minas, and Menedora; and if he owes me anything I acquit him of the debt. And I give to Hilaras four minae, and a double carpet, and two pillows, and a curtain, and any couch which he chooses to select. I also hereby emancipate the mother of Micras, and Noemon, and Dion, and Theon, and Euphranor, and Hermeas; and I desire that Agathon shall have his freedom when he has served two years longer; and that Ophelion, and Poseideon, my litter-bearers, shall have theirs when they have waited four years more. I also give to Demetrius, and Criton, and Syrus, a couch a piece, and coverlets from those which I leave behind me, according to the selection which Lycon is hereby authorized to make.

And these are to be their rewards for having performed the duties to which they were appointed well. Concerning my burial, let Lycon do as he pleases, and bury me here or at home, just as he likes; for I am sure that he has the same regard for propriety that I myself have. And I give all the things herein mentioned, in the confidence that he will arrange everything properly. The witnesses to this my will are Callinus of Hermione, Ariston of Ceos, and Euphronius of Pseania."

As he then was thoroughly wise in everything relating to education, and every branch of philosophy, he was no less prudent and careful in the framing of his will. So that in this respect to he deserves to be admired and imitated.

The Aristotelian Sense of Proportion by William Hyde

I: ARISTOTLE'S OBJECTIONS TO PREVIOUS SYSTEMS

Our principles of personality thus far, though increasingly complex, have all been comparatively simple. To get the maximum of pleasure; to keep the universal law; to subordinate lower impulses to higher according to some fixed scale of value, are all principles which are easy to grasp and by no means difficult to apply. The fundamental trouble with them all is that they are too easy. Life is not the cut-and-dried affair which they presuppose. A man might have a lot of pleasure, and yet be contemptible. He might keep all the commandments, and yet be no better than a Pharisee. Even Plato's principle in actual practice has not always escaped the awful abyss of asceticism.

In opposition to Epicurus Aristotle says, "Pleasure is not the good and all pleasures are not desirable. No one would choose to live on condition of having no more intellect than a child all his life, even though he were to enjoy to the full the pleasures of a child. With regard to the pleasures which all admit to be base, we must deny that they are pleasures at all, except to those whose nature is corrupt. What the good man thinks is pleasure will be pleasure; what he delights in will be truly pleasant. Those pleasures which perfect the activity of the perfect and truly happy man may be called in the truest sense the pleasures of a man. The pleasure which is proper to a good activity is therefore good; that attached to a bad one is bad. As, then, activities differ, so do the pleasures which accompany them."

In our discussion of Epicureanism we saw that the principle of pleasure consistently carried out produced bad results, and, as in the case of Tito Melema, developed the most contemptible character. Aristotle shows conclusively why this must be so. Pleasure is the sign and seal of healthful exercise of function. A life which has all its powers in effective and well-proportioned exercise will, indeed, be a life crowned with pleasure. You cannot, however, reverse this proposition, as the Epicurean attempts to do, and say that a life which seeks the maximum of pleasure will inevitably have the healthy and proportionate exercise of function as its consequent. According to Aristotle healthy exercise of function in a well-proportioned life in devotion to wide social ends and permanent personal interests, is the cause of which happiness is the appropriate and inevitable effect. Seek the cause and you will get the effect. Seek directly the effect, and you will miss both the cause you neglect and the effect which only the cause can bring. The criticism which we quoted from George Eliot on the career of Melema is the quintessence of the Aristotelian doctrine. To put it in a figure: Build a good fire and warm your room, and the mercury in the thermometer will rise. The cause produces the effect. But it does not follow that because you raise the mercury in the thermometer by breathing on the bulb, or holding it in your hand, that the fire will burn, or the room will be warmed. The Epicureans and hedonists are people who go about with the clinical thermometer of pleasure under their tongues all the time, and expect to see the world lighted with benevolence and warmed with love in consequence. Aristotle bids them take their clinical thermometers out of their mouths; stop fingering their emotional pulse; go to work about some useful business; pursue some large and generous end; and then, not otherwise, in case from time to time they have occasion to feel their pulse and take their temperature, they will as a matter of fact find that they are normal. But it isn't taking the temperature and feeling the pulse that makes them morally sound; it is doing their proper work and keeping in vigorous exercise that gives them the healthy pulse and normal temperature.

There are, however, two apparently contradictory teachings about pleasure in Aristotle, and it is a good test of our grasp of his doctrine to see whether we can reconcile them. First he says, "In all cases we must be especially on our guard against pleasant things, and against pleasure; for we can scarce judge her impartially. And so, in our behaviour toward her, we should imitate the behaviour of the old counsellors toward Helen, and in all cases repeat their saying: If we dismiss her, we shall be less likely to go wrong." "It is pleasure that moves us to do what is base, and pain that moves us to refrain from what is noble."

On the other hand he says: "The pleasure or pain that accompanies the acts must be taken as a test of character. He who faces danger with pleasure, or, at any rate, without pain, is courageous, but he to whom this is painful is a coward. Indeed we all more or less make pleasure our test in judging actions."

Can we reconcile these two seemingly contradictory statements? Perfectly. On the one hand if we do an act simply for the pleasure it will give, without first asking how the proposed act will fit into our permanent plan of life, we are pretty sure to go astray. For pleasure registers the goodness of the isolated act; not the goodness of the act as related to the whole plan of life. Thus if I drink strong coffee at eleven o'clock at night, the taste is pleasant and the immediate effect is stimulating. But if it keeps me awake half the night and unfits me for the duties of the next day, in spite of the pleasure gained, the act is wrong. And it is wrong, not fundamentally because of the pains of wakefulness it brings; it is wrong because it takes out of my life as a whole, and my contribution to the life of the world, something for which the petty transient pleasure I gained at the moment of indulindulgence is no compensation whatsoever. Is not Aristotle right? Do we not pity as a miserable weakling, hardly fit to have been graduated from the nursery, any man or woman who will let the mere physical sensation of a few moments at the end of an evening count so much as the dust in the balance against the efficiency of the coming forenoon's life and work?

If we see this half of Aristotle's truth, we see that the other is not its contradiction but its complement. If we are sorely and grievously tempted by the coffee, if we give it up with pain, if saying "No, I thank you," comes fearfully hard, if we cannot forego it cheerfully without so much as seriously considering the drinking of it as possible for us, why then it reveals how little we care for the life and work of the morrow; and since life and work are but a succession of to-morrows, how little we care for our life and work anyway. If we had great aims burning in our minds and hearts, wide interests to which body and soul were devoted, it would not be a pain, it would be a pleasure, to give up for the sake of them ten thousand times as big a thing as a cup of coffee, if it stood in the way of their accomplishment. Yes; Aristotle is right on both points. Pleasure isolated from our plan of life and followed as an end will lead us into weakness and wickedness every time we yield to its insidious solicitation. On the other hand, the resolute and consistent prosecution of large ends and generous interests will make a positive pleasure of everything we either endure or do to promote those ends and interests. Pleasure directly pursued is the utter demoralisation of life. Ends and interests, pursued for their own sakes, inevitably carry with them a host of noble pleasures, and the power to conquer and transform what to the aimless life would be intolerable pains.

Aristotle rejects the Epicurean principle of pleasure; because, though a proof that isolated tendencies are satisfied, it is no adequate criterion of the satisfaction of the self as a whole. He rejects the Stoic principle of conformity to law; because it fails to recognise the supreme worth of individuality. He rejects the Platonic principle of subordination of appetites and passions to a supreme good which is above them; because he dreads above all things the blight of asceticism, and strives for a good which is concrete and practical.

What, then, is this good, which is neither a sum of pleasures, nor conformity to law; nor yet superiority to appetite and passion? What is this principle which can at once enjoy pleasure to the full, and at the same time forego it gladly; which can make laws for itself more severe than any lawgiver ever dared to lay down; and yet is not afraid to break any law which its own conception of good requires it to break; which honours all our elemental appetites and passions, uses money and honour and power as the servants of its own ends, without ever being enslaved by them? Evidently we are now on the track of a principle infinitely more subtle and complex than anything the pleasure-loving Epicurean, or the formal Stoic, or the transcendental Platonist has ever dreamed of. We are entering the presence of the world's master moralist; and if we have ever for a moment supposed that either of these previous systems was satisfactory or final, it behooves us now to take the shoes from off our feet, and reverently listen to a voice as much profounder and more reasonable than them all, as they are superior to the senseless appetites and blind passions of the mob. For if we have a little patience with his subtlety, and can endure the temporary shock of his apparent laxity, he will admit us to the very holy of holies of personality.

II: THE SOCIAL NATURE OF MAN

Before coming to Aristotle's positive doctrine we must consider one fundamental axiom.
Man is by nature a social being.
Whatever a man seeks has a necessary and inevitable reference to the judgment of other men, and the interest of society as a whole. Strip a man of his relations and you have no man left. The man who is neither son, brother, husband, father, citizen, neighbour or workman, is inconceivable. The good which a man seeks, therefore, will express itself consciously or unconsciously in terms of other men's approval, and the furtherance of interests which he inevitably shares with them. The Greek word for private, peculiar to myself, unrelated to the thought or interest of anybody else, is our word for idiot. The New Testament uses this word to describe the place to which Judas went; a place which just suited such a man as he, and was fit for nobody else. Now a man who tries to be his own scientist, or his own lawgiver, or his own statesman, or his own business manager, or his own poet, or his own architect, without reference to the standards and expectations of his fellow-men, is just an idiot; or, as we say, a "crank." A wise man may defy these standards. The reformer often must do so. But if he is really wise, if he is a true reformer, he must reckon with them; he must understand them; he must appeal to the actual or possible judgment and interest of his fellows for the confirmation of what he says and the justification of what he does. This social reference of all our thoughts and actions, which Aristotle grasped by intuition, psychology in our day is laboriously and analytically seeking to

confirm. Aristotle lays it down as an axiom, that a man who does not devote himself to some section of the social and spiritual world, if such a being were conceivable, would be no man at all. Family, or friends, or reputation, or country, or God are there in the background, secretly summoned to justify our every thought and word and deed.

Because man's nature is social, his end must be social also. It will prevent misunderstanding later, if we put the question squarely here, Does the end justify the means? As popularly understood, most emphatically No. The support of a school is a good end. Does it justify the raising of money by a lottery? Certainly not. The support of one's family is a good end. Does it justify drawing a salary for which no adequate services are rendered? Certainly not.

Yet if we push the question farther, and ask why these particular ends do not justify these particular means, we discover that it is because these means employed are destructive of an end vastly higher and greater than the particular ends they are employed to serve. They break down the structure and undermine the foundations of the industrial and social order; an end infinitely more important than the maintenance of any particular school, or the support of any individual family. Hence these means are not to be judged by their promotion of certain specific ends, but by their failure to promote the greatest and best end of all; the comprehensive welfare of society as a whole, of which all institutions and families and individuals are but subordinate members.

Throughout our discussion of Aristotle we must understand that the word "end" always has this large social reference, and includes the highest social service of which the man is capable. If we attempt to apply to particular private ends of our own what Aristotle applies to the universal end at which all men ought to aim, we shall make his teaching a pretext for the grossest crimes, and reduce it to little more than sophisticated selfishness. With this understanding of his terms, we may venture to plunge boldly into his system and state it in its most paradoxical and startling form.

III: RIGHT AND WRONG DETERMINED BY THE END

We are not either good or bad at the start. Pleasure in itself is neither good nor bad. Laws in themselves are neither good nor bad. It is impossible to say with Plato that some faculties are so high that they always ought to be exercised, and others are so low that as a rule they ought to be suppressed. The right and wrong of eating and drinking, of work and play, of sex and society, of property and politics, lie not in the elemental acts involved. All of these things are right for one man in one set of circumstances, wrong for another man in another set of circumstances. We cannot say that a man who takes a vow of poverty is either a better or a worse man than a multi-millionaire. We cannot say that the monk who takes a vow of celibacy is a purer man than one who does not. For the very fact that one is compelled to take a vow of poverty or celibacy is a sign that these elemental impulses are not effectively and satisfactorily related to the normal ends they are naturally intended to subserve. All attempts to put virginity above motherhood, to put poverty above riches, to put obscurity above fame are, from the Aristotelian point of view, essentially immoral. For they all assume that there can be badness in external things, wrong in isolated actions, vice in elemental appetites, and sin in natural passions; whereas Aristotle lays down the fundamental principle that the only place where either badness or wrong or vice or sin can reside is in the relation in which these external things and particular actions stand to the clearly conceived and deliberately cherished end which the man is seeking to promote. A simpler way of saying the same thing, but a way so simple and familiar as to be in danger of missing the whole point, is to say that virtue and vice reside exclusively in the wills of free agents. That, every one will admit. But will is the pursuit of ends. A will that seeks no ends is a will that wills nothing; in other words, no will at all. Whether an act is wrong or right, then, depends on the whole plan of life of which it is a part; on the relation in which it stands to one's permanent interests. For these many years I have defied class after class of college students to bring in a single example of any elemental appetite or passion which is intrinsically bad; which in all circumstances and relations is evil. And never yet has any student brought me one such case. If brandy will tide the weak heart over the crisis that follows a surgical operation, then that glass of brandy is just as good and precious as the dear life it saves. The proposition that sexual love is intrinsically evil, and those who take vows of celibacy are intrinsically superior, is true only on condition that racial suicide is the greatest good, and all the sweet ties of home and family and parenthood and brotherly love are evils which it is our duty to combat. To deny that wealth is good is only possible to him who is prepared to go farther and denounce civilisation as a calamity. He who brands ambition as intrinsically evil must be prepared to herd with swine, and share contentedly their fare of husks.

The foundation of personality, therefore, is the power to clearly grasp an imaginary condition of ourselves which is preferable to any practical alternative; and then translate that potential picture into an accomplished fact. Whoever lives at a lower level than this constant translation of pictured potency into energetic reality: whoever, seeing the picture of the self he wants to be, suffers aught less noble and less imperative than that to determine his action misses the mark of personality. Whoever sees the picture, and holds it before his mind so clearly that all external things which favour it are chosen for its sake, and all proposed actions which would hinder it are remorselessly rejected in its holy name and by its mighty power;—he rises to the level of personality, and his personality is of that clear, strong, joyous, compelling, conquering, triumphant sort which alone is worthy of the name.

How much deeper this goes than anything we have had before! A man comes up for judgment. If Epicurus chances to be seated on the throne, he asks the candidate, "Have you had a good time?" If he has, he opens the gates of Paradise; if he has not, he bids him be off to the place of torment where people who don't know how to enjoy themselves ought to go.

The Stoic asks him whether he has kept all the commandments. If he has, then he may be promoted to serve the great Commander in other departments of the cosmic order. If he has broken the least of them, no matter on what pretext, or under what temptation, he is irrevocably doomed. Plato asks him how well he has managed to keep under his appetites and passions. If the man has risen above them, Plato will promote him to seats nearer the perfect goodness of the gods. If he has slipped or failed, then he must return for longer probation in the prison-house of sense.

Aristotle's judgment seat is a very different place. A man comes to him who has had a very sorry time: who has broken many commandments; who has yielded time and again to sensuous desires; yet who is a good husband, a kind father, an honest workman, a loyal citizen, a disinterested scientist or artist, a lover of his fellows, a worshipper of God's beauty and beneficence; and in spite of the sad time he has had, in spite of the laws he has broken, in spite of the appetites which have proved too strong for him, Aristotle gives him his hand, and bids him go up higher. For that man stands in genuine relations to some aspects of the great social end to which he devotes himself. And because some portion of the real world has been made better by the conception of it he has cherished, and the fidelity with which he has translated his conception into fact, therefore a share in the great glory of the splendid whole belongs of right to him. Good honest work, after an ideal plan, to the full measure of his powers, with wise selection of appropriate means, gives each individual his place and rank in the vast workshop wherein the eternal thoughts of God, revealed to men as their several ideals, are wrought out into the actuality of the social, economic, political, æsthetic and spiritual order of the world.

On the other hand, the man of scattered and unfruitful pleasures, the man of merely clear conscience, pure life, unstained reputation, with his boast of rites observed, and ceremonies performed, and laws unbroken, "faultily faultless, icily regular, splendidly null," is the man above all others whom Aristotle cannot endure.

Do you wish, then, to know precisely where you stand in the scale of personality? Here is the test. How large a section of this world do you care for, in such a vital, responsible way, that you are thinking about its welfare, forming schemes for its improvement, bending your energies toward its advancement? Do you care for your profession in that way? Do you care for your family like that? Do you love your country with such jealous solicitude for its honour and prosperity? Can you honestly say that your neighbour gets represented in your mind in this imaginative, sympathetic, helpful way? Do you think of God's great universe as something in the goodness of which you rejoice, and for the welfare of which you are earnestly enlisted? Begin down at the bottom, with your stomach, your pocket-book, your calling list, and go up the scale until you come to these wider interests, and mark the point where you cease to think how these things might be better than they are and to work to make them so, and that point where your imagination and your service stops, and your indifference and irresponsibility begins, will show you precisely how you stand on the rank-book of God. The magnitude of the ends you see and serve is the measure of your personality. Personality is not an entity we carry around in our spiritual pockets. It is an energy, which is no whit larger or smaller than the ends it aims at and the work it does. If you are not doing anything or caring for anybody, or devoted to any end, you will not be called up at some future time and formally punished for your negligence. Plato might flatter your self-importance with that notion, but not Aristotle. Aristotle tells you, not that your soul will be punished hereafter, but that it is lost already.

Goodness does not consist in doing or refraining from doing this or that particular thing. It depends on the whole aim and purpose of the man who does it, or refrains from doing it. Anything which a good man does as part of the best plan of life is made thereby a good act. And anything that a bad man does, as part of a bad plan of life, becomes thereby an evil act. Precisely the same external act is good for one man and bad for another. An example or two will make this clear.

Two men seek political office. For one man it is the gate of heaven; to the other it is the door to hell. One man has established himself in a business or profession in which he can earn an honest living and support his family. He has acquired sufficient standing in his business so that he can turn it over temporarily to his partners or subordinates. He has solved his own problem; and he has strength, time, energy, capacity, money, which he can give to solving the problems of the public. Were he to shirk public office, or evade it, or fail to take all legitimate means to secure it, he would be a coward, a traitor, a parasite on the body politic. For there is good work to be done, which he is able to do, and can afford to do, without unreasonable sacrifice of himself or his family. Hence public office is for this man the gateway of heaven.

The other man has not mastered any business or profession; he has not made himself indispensable to any employer or firm; he has no permanent means of supporting himself and his family. He sees a political office in which he can get a little more salary for doing a good deal less work than is possible in his present position. He seeks the office, as a means of getting his living out of the public. From that day forth he joins the horde of mere office-seekers, aiming to get out of the public a living he is too lazy, or too incompetent, or too proud to earn in private employment. Thus the very same external act, which was the other man's strait, narrow gateway to heaven, is for this man the broad, easy descent into hell.

Two women join the same woman's club, and take part in the same programme. One of them has her heart in her home; has fulfilled all the sweet charities of daughter, sister, wife, or mother; and in order to bring back to these loved ones at home wider interests, larger friendships, and a richer and more varied interest in life, has gone out into the work and life of the club. No angel in heaven is better employed than she in the preparation and delivery of her papers and her attendance on committee meetings and afternoon teas.

The other woman finds home life dull and monotonous. She likes to get away from her children. She craves excitement, flattery, fame, social importance. She is restless, irritable, out of sorts, censorious, complaining at home; animated, gracious, affable, complaisant abroad. For drudgery and duty she has no strength, taste, or talent; and the thought of these things are enough to give her dyspepsia, insomnia, and nervous prostration. But for all sorts of public functions, for the preparation of reports, and the organisation of new charitable and philanthropic and social schemes, she has all the energy of a steam-engine, the power of a dynamo. When this woman joins a new club, or writes a new paper, or gets a new office, though she does not a single thing more than her angel sister who sits by her side, she is playing the part of a devil.

It is not what one does; it is the whole purpose of life consciously or unconsciously expressed in the doing that measures the worth of the man or woman who does it. At the family table, at the bench in the shop, at the desk in the office, in the seats at the theatre, in the ranks of the army, in the pews of the church, saint and sinner sit side by side; and often the keenest outward observer cannot detect the slightest difference in the particular things that they do. The good man is he who, in each act he does or refrains from doing, is seeking the good of all the persons who are affected by his action. The bad man is the man who, whatever he does or refrains from doing, leaves out of account the interests of some of the people whom his action is sure to affect. Is there any sphere of human welfare to which you are indifferent? Are there any people in the world whose interests you deliberately disregard? Then, no matter how many acts of charity and philanthropy, and industry and public spirit you perform—acts which would be good if a good man did them—in spite of them all, you are to that extent an evil man.

We have, then, clearly in mind Aristotle's first great concept. The end of life, which he calls happiness, he defines as the identification of one's self with some large social or intellectual object, and the devotion of all one's powers to its disinterested service. So far forth it is Carlyle's gospel of the blessedness of work in a worthy cause. "Blessed is he who has found his work; let him ask no other blessedness. He has a work, a life purpose; he has found it, and will follow it. The only happiness a brave man ever troubled himself with asking much about was happiness enough to get his work done. Whatsoever of morality and of intelligence; what of patience, perseverance, faithfulness of method, insight, ingenuity, energy; in a word, whatsoever of strength the man had in him will lie written in the work he does. To work: why, it is to try himself against Nature and her everlasting unerring laws; these will tell a true verdict as to the man."

When we read Carlyle, we are apt to think such words merely exaggerated rhetoric. Now Aristotle says the same thing in the cold, calculated terms of precise philosophy. A man is what he does. He can do nothing except what he first sees as an unaccomplished idea, and then bends all his energies to accomplish. In working out his ideas and making them real, he at the same time works out his own powers, and becomes a living force, a working will in the world. And since the soul is just this working will, the man has so much soul, no more, no less, than he registers in manual or mental work performed. To be able to point to some sphere of external reality, a bushel of corn, a web of cloth, a printed page, a healthful tenement, an educated youth, a moral community, and say that these things would not have been there in the outward world, if they had not first been in your mind as an idea controlling your thought and action;—this is to point to the external and visible counterpart and measure of the invisible and internal energy which is your life, your soul, your self, your personality.

IV: THE NEED OF INSTRUMENTS

Aristotle's first doctrine, then, is that we must work for worthy ends. The second follows directly from it. We must have tools to work with; means by which to gain our ends. General Gordon, who was something of a Platonist, remarked to Cecil Rhodes, who was a good deal of an Aristotelian, that he once had a whole room full of gold offered him, and declined to take it. "I should have taken it," replied Mr. Rhodes. "What is the use of having great schemes if you haven't the means to carry them out?" As Aristotle says: "Happiness plainly requires external goods; for it is impossible, or at least not easy, to act nobly without some furniture of fortune. There are many things that can be done only through instruments, so to speak, such as friends and wealth and political influence; and there are some things whose absence takes the bloom off our happiness, as good birth, the blessing of children, personal beauty. Happiness, then, seems to stand in need of this kind of prosperity."

How different this from all our previous teachings! The Epicurean wants little wealth, no family, no official station; because all these things involve so much care and bother. The Stoic barely tolerates them as indifferent. Plato took especial pains to deprive his guardians of most of these very things. Aristotle on this point is perfectly sane. He says you want them; because, to the fullest life and the largest work, they are well-nigh indispensable. The editor of a metropolitan newspaper, the president of a railroad, the corporation attorney cannot live their lives and do their work effectively without comfortable homes, enjoyable vacations, social connections, educational opportunities, which cost a great deal of money. For them to despise money would be to despise the conditions of their own effective living, to pour contempt on their own souls.

Is Aristotle, then, a gross materialist, a mere money-getter, pleasure-lover, office-seeker? Far from it. These things are not the end of a noble life, but means by which to serve ends far worthier than themselves. To make these things the ends of life, he explicitly says is shameful and unnatural. The good, the true end, is "something which is a man's own, and cannot be taken away from him."

Now we have two fundamental Aristotelian doctrines. We must have an end, some section of the world which we undertake to mould according to a pattern clearly seen and firmly grasped in our own minds.

Second, we must have instruments, tools, furniture of fortune in the shape of health, wealth, influence, power, friends, business and social and political connections with which to carry out our ends. And the larger and nobler our ends, the more of these instruments shall we require. If, like Cecil

Rhodes, we undertake for instance to paint the map of Africa British red, we shall want a monopoly of the product of the Kimberley and adjacent diamond mines.

V: THE HAPPY MEAN

The third great Aristotelian principle follows directly from these two. If we are to use instruments for some great end, then the amount of the instruments we want, and the extent to which we shall use them, will obviously be determined by the end at which we aim. We must take just so much of them as will best promote that end. This is Aristotle's much misunderstood but most characteristic doctrine of the mean. Approached from the point of view which we have already gained, this doctrine of the mean is perfectly intelligible, and altogether reasonable. For instance, if you are an athlete, and the winning of a foot-ball game is your end, and you have an invitation to a ball the evening before the game, what is the right and reasonable thing to do? Dancing in itself is good. You enjoy it. You would like to go. You need recreation after the long period of training. But if you are wise, you will decline. Why? Because the excitement of the ball, the late hours, the physical effort, the nervous expenditure will use up more energy than can be recovered before the game comes off upon the morrow. You decline, not because the ball is an intrinsic evil, or dancing is intrinsically bad, or recreation is inherently injurious, but because too much of these things, in the precise circumstances in which you are placed, with the specific end you have in view, would be disastrous. On the other hand, will you have no recreation the evening before the game; but simply sit in your room and mope? That would be even worse than going to the ball. For nature abhors a vacuum in the mind no less than in the world of matter. If you sit alone in your room, you will begin to worry about the game, and very likely lose your night's sleep, and be utterly unfitted when the time arrives. Too little recreation in these circumstances is as fatal as too much. What you want is just enough to keep your mind pleasantly diverted, without effort or exertion on your part. If the glee club can be brought around to sing some jolly songs, if a funny man can be found to tell amusing stories, you have the happy mean; that is, just enough recreation to put you in condition for a night's sound sleep, and bring you to the contest on the morrow in prime physical and mental condition.

Aristotle, in his doctrine of the mean, is simply telling us that this problem of the athlete on the night before the contest is the personal problem of us all every day of our lives.

How late shall the student study at night? Shall he keep on until past midnight year after year? If he does, he will undermine his health, lose contact with society, and defeat those ends of social usefulness which ought to be part of every worthy scholar's cherished end. On the other hand, shall he fritter away all his evenings with convivial fellows, and the society butterflies? Too much of that sort of thing would soon put an end to scholarship altogether. His problem is to find that amount of study which will keep him sensitively alive to the latest problems of his chosen subject; and yet not make all his acquisitions comparatively worthless either through broken health, or social estrangement from his fellow-men. How rare and precious that mean is, those of us who have to find college professors are well aware. It is easy to find scores of men who know their subject so well that they know nothing and nobody else aright. It is easy to find jolly, easy-going fellows who would not object to positions as college professors. But the man who has enough good fellowship and physical vigour to make his scholarship attractive and effective, and enough scholarship to make his vigour and good fellowship intellectually powerful and personally stimulating,—he is the man who has hit the Aristotelian mean; he is the man we are all after; he is the man whom we would any of us give a year's salary to find.

The mean is not midway between zero and the maximum attainable. As Aristotle says, "By the mean relatively to us I understand that which is neither too much nor too little for us; and that is not one and the same for all. For instance, if ten be too large and two be too small, if we take six, we take the mean relatively to the thing itself, or the arithmetical mean. But the mean relatively to us cannot be found in this way. If ten pounds of food is too much for a given man to eat, and two pounds too little, it does not follow that the trainer will order him six pounds; for that also may perhaps be too much for the man in question, or too little; too little for Milo, too much for the beginner. And so we may say generally that a master in any art avoids what is too much and what is too little, and seeks for the mean and chooses it—not the absolute but the relative mean. So that people are wont to say of a good work, that nothing could be taken from it or added to it, implying that excellence is destroyed by excess or deficiency, but secured by observing the mean."

The Aristotelian principle, of judging a situation on its merits, and subordinating means to the supreme end, was never more clearly stated than in Lincoln's letter to Horace Greeley: "I would save the Union. If there be those who would not save the Union unless they could at the same time save slavery, I do not agree with them. If there be those who would not save the Union unless they could at the same time destroy slavery, I do not agree with them. My paramount object in this struggle is to save the Union, and is not either to save or to destroy slavery. If I could save the Union without freeing any slave, I would do it; and if I could save it by freeing all the slaves, I would do it; and if I could save it by freeing some and leaving others alone, I would do that. What I do about slavery and the coloured race, I do because I believe it helps to save the Union; and what I forbear, I forbear because I do not believe it would help to save the Union. I shall do less whenever I believe what I am doing hurts the cause, and I shall do more when I shall believe doing more will help the cause."

VI: THE ARISTOTELIAN VIRTUES AND THEIR ACQUISITION

The special forms that the one great virtue of seeking the relative mean takes in actual life bear a close correspondence to the cardinal virtues of Plato; yet with a difference which marks a positive advance in insight. Aristotle, to begin with, distinguishes wisdom from prudence. Wisdom is the theoretic knowledge of things as they are, irrespective of their serviceableness to our practical interests. In modern terms it is devotion to pure science. This corresponds to Plato's contemplation of the Good. According to Aristotle this devotion to knowledge for its own sake underlies all virtue; for only he who knows how things stand related to each other in the actual world, will be able to grasp aright that relation of means to ends on which the success of the practical life depends. Just as the engineer cannot build a bridge across the Mississippi unless he knows those laws of pure mathematics and physics which underlie the stability of all structures, so the man who is ignorant of economics, politics, sociology, psychology, and ethics is sure to make a botch of any attempts he may make to build bridges across the gulf which separates one man from another man; one group of citizens from another group. Pure science is at the basis of all art, consciously or unconsciously; and therefore wisdom is the fundamental form of virtue.

Prudence comes next; the power to see, not the theoretical relations of men and things to each other, but the practical relationships of men and things to our self-chosen ends. Wisdom knows the laws which govern the strength of materials. Prudence knows how strong a structure is necessary to support the particular strain we wish to place upon it. Wisdom knows sociology. Prudence tells us whether in a given case it is better to give a beggar a quarter of a dollar, an order on a central bureau, a scolding, or a kick. The most essential, and yet the rarest kind of prudence is that considerateness which sensitively appreciates the point of view of the people with whom we deal, and takes proper account of those subtle and complex sentiments, prejudices, traditions, and ways of thinking, which taken together constitute the social situation.

Temperance, again, is not the repression of lower impulses in the interest of those abstractly higher, as it came to be in the popular interpretations of Platonism, and as it was in Stoicism. With Aristotle it is the stern and remorseless exclusion of whatever cannot be brought into subjection to my chosen ends, whatever they may be. As Stevenson says in true Aristotelian spirit, "We are not damned for doing wrong: we are damned for not doing right." For temperance lies not in the external thing done or left undone, but in that relation of means to worthy ends which either the doing or the not doing of certain things may most effectively express. We shall never get any common basis of understanding on what we call the temperance question of to-day until we learn to recognise this internal and moral, as distinct from the external and physical, definition of what true temperance is. Temperance isn't abstinence. Temperance isn't indulgence. Neither is it moderation in the ordinary sense of that term. True temperance is the using of just so much of a thing,—no more, no less, but just so much,—as best promotes the ends one has at heart. To discover whether a man is temperate or not in anything, you must first know the ends at which he aims; and then the strictness with which he uses the means that best further those ends, and foregoes the things that would hinder them.

Temperance of this kind looks at first sight like license. So it is if one's aims be not broad and high. In the matter of sexual morality, Aristotle's doctrine as applied in his day was notoriously loose. Whatever did not interfere with one's duties as citizen and soldier was held to be permissible. Yet as Green and Muirhead, and all the commentators on Aristotle have pointed out, it is a deeper grasp of this very principle of Aristotle, a widening of the conception of the true social end, which is destined to put chastity on its eternal rock foundation, and make of sexual immorality the transparently weak and wanton, cruel and unpardonable vice it is. To do this, to be sure, there must be grafted on to it the Christian principle of democracy,—a regard for the rights and interests of persons as persons. The beauty of the Aristotelian principle is that it furnishes so stout and sturdy a stock to graft this principle on to. When Christianity is unsupported by some such solid trunk of rationality, it easily drops into a sentimental asceticism. Take, for example, this very matter of sexual morality. Divorced from some such great social end as Aristotelianism requires, the only defence you have against the floods of sensuality is the vague, sentimental, ascetic notion that in some way or other these things are naughty, and good people ought not to do them. How utterly ineffective such a barrier is, everybody who has had much dealing with young men knows perfectly well. And yet that is pretty much all the opposition current and conventional morality is offering at the present time. The Aristotelian doctrine, with the Christian principle grafted on, puts two plain questions to every man. Do you include the sanctity of the home, the peace and purity of family life, the dignity and welfare of every man and woman, the honest birthright of every child, as part of the social end at which you aim? If you do, you are a noble and honourable man. If you do not, then you are a disgrace to the mother who bore you, and the home where you were reared. So much for the question of the end. The second question is concerned with the means. Do you honestly believe that loose and promiscuous sexual relations conduce to that sanctity of the home, that peace and purity of family life, that dignity and welfare of every man and woman, that honest birthright of every child, which as an honourable man you must admit to be the proper end at which to aim? If you think these means are conducive to these ends, then you are certainly an egregious fool. Temperance in these matters, then, or to use its specific name, chastity, is simply the refusal to ignore the great social end which every decent man must recognise as reasonable and right; and the resolute determination not to admit into his own life, or inflict on the lives of others, anything that is destructive of that social end. Chastity is neither celibacy nor licentiousness. It is far deeper than either, and far nobler than them both. It is devotion to the great ends of family integrity, personal dignity, and social stability. It is including the welfare of society, and of every man, woman, and child involved, in the comprehensive end for which we live; and holding all appetites and passions in strict relation to that reasonable and righteous end.

Aristotelian courage is simply the other side of temperance. Temperance remorselessly cuts off whatever hinders the ends at which we aim. Courage, on the other hand, resolutely takes on whatever dangers and losses, whatever pains and penalties are incidental to the effective prosecution of these ends. To hold consistently an end, is to endure cheerfully whatever means the service of that end demands. Aristotelian courage, rightly conceived, leads us to the very threshold of Christian sacrifice. He who comes to Christian sacrifice by this approach of Aristotelian courage, will be perfectly clear about the reasonableness of it, and will escape that abyss of sentimentalism into which too largely our Christian doctrine of sacrifice has been allowed to drop.

Courage does not depend on whether you save your life, or risk your life, or lose your life. A brave man may save his life in situations where a coward would lose it and a fool would risk it. The brave man is he who is so clear and firm in his grasp of some worthy end that he will live if he can best serve it by living; that he will die if he can best serve it by dying; and he will take his chances of life or death if taking those chances is the best way to serve this end.

The brave man does not like criticism, unpopularity, defeat, hostility, any better than anybody else. He does not pretend to like them. He does not court them. He does not pose as a martyr every chance that he can get. He simply takes these pains and ills as under the circumstances the best means of furthering the ends he has at heart. For their sake he swallows criticism and calls it good; invites opposition and glories in overcoming it, or being overcome by it, as the fates may decree; accepts persecution and rejoices to be counted worthy to suffer in so good a cause.

It is all a question here as everywhere in Aristotle of the ends at which one aims, and the sense of proportion with which he chooses his means. In his own words: "The man, then, who governs his fear and likewise his confidence aright, facing dangers it is right to face, and for the right cause, in the right manner, and at the right time, is courageous. For the courageous man regulates both his feelings and his actions with due regard to the circumstances and as reason and proportion suggest. The courageous man, therefore, faces danger and does the courageous thing because it is a fine thing to do." As Muirhead sums up Aristotle's teaching on this point: "True courage must be for a noble object. Here, as in all excellence, action and object, consequence and motive, are inseparable. Unless the action is inspired by a noble motive, and permeated throughout its whole structure by a noble character, it has no claim to the name of courage."

The virtues cannot be learned out of a book, or picked up ready-made. They must be acquired, by practice, as is the case with the arts; and they are not really ours until they have become so habitual as to be practically automatic. The sign and seal of the complete acquisition of any virtue is the pleasure we take in it. Such pleasure once gained becomes one's lasting and inalienable possession.

In Aristotle's words: "We acquire the virtues by doing the acts, as is the case with the arts too. We learn an art by doing that which we wish to do when we have learned it; we become builders by building, and harpers by playing on the harp. And so by doing just acts we become just, and by doing acts of temperance and courage we become temperate and courageous. It is by our conduct in our intercourse with other men that we become just or unjust, and by acting in circumstances of danger, and training ourselves to feel fear or confidence, that we become courageous or cowardly." "The happy man, then, as we define him, will have the property of permanence, and all through life will preserve his character; for he will be occupied continually, or with the least possible interruption, in excellent deeds and excellent speculations; and whatever his fortune may be, he will take it in the noblest fashion, and bear himself always and in all things suitably. And if it is what man does that determines the character of his life, then no happy man will become miserable, for he will never do what is hateful and base. For we hold that the man who is truly good and wise will bear with dignity whatever fortune sends, and will always make the best of his circumstances, as a good general will turn the forces at his command to the best account."

This doctrine that virtue, like skill in any game or craft, is gained by practice, deserves a word of comment. It seems to say, "You must do the thing before you know how, in order to know how after you have done it." Paradox or no paradox, that is precisely the fact. The swimmer learns to swim by floundering and splashing around in the water; and if he is unwilling to do the floundering and splashing before he can swim, he will never become a swimmer. The ball-player must do a lot of muffing and wild throwing before he can become a sure catcher and a straight thrower. If he is ashamed to go out on the diamond and make these errors, he may as well give up at once all idea of ever becoming a ball-player. For it is by the progressive elimination of errors that the perfect player is developed. The only place where no errors are made, whether in base-ball or in life, is on the grand stand. The courage to try to do a thing before you know how, and the patience to keep on trying after you have found out that you don't know how, and the perseverance to renew the trial as many times as necessary until you do know how, are the three conditions of the acquisition of physical skill, mental power, moral virtue, or personal excellence.

VII: ARISTOTELIAN FRIENDSHIP

We are now prepared to see why Aristotle regards friendship as the crown and consummation of a virtuous life. No one has praised friendship more highly, or written of it more profoundly than he.

Friendship he defines as "unanimity on questions of the public advantage and on all that touches life." This unanimity, however, is very different from agreement in opinion. It is seeing things from the same point of view; or, more accurately, it is the appreciation of each other's interests and aims. The whole tendency of Aristotle thus far has been to develop individuality; to make each man different from every other man. Conventional people are all alike. But the people who have cherished ends of their own, and who make all their choices with reference to these inwardly cherished ends, become highly differentiated. The more individual your life becomes, the fewer people there are who can understand you. The man who has ends of his own is bound to be unintelligible to the man who has no such ends, and is merely drifting with the crowd. Now friendship is the bringing together of these intensely individual, highly differentiated persons on a basis of mutual sympathy and common understanding. Friendship is the recognition and respect of individuality in others by persons who are highly individualised themselves. That is why Aristotle says true friendship is possible only between the good; between people, that is, who are in earnest about ends that are large and generous and public-spirited enough to permit of being shared. "The bad," he says, "desire the company of others, but avoid their own. And because they avoid their own company, there is no real basis for union of aims and interests with their fellows." "Having nothing lovable about them, they have no friendly feelings toward themselves. If such a condition is consummately miserable, the moral is to shun vice, and strive after virtue with all one's might. For in this way we shall at once have friendly feelings toward ourselves and become the friends of others. A good man stands in the same relation to his friend as to himself, seeing that his friend is a second self." "The conclusion, therefore, is that if a man is to be happy, he will require good friends."

Friendship has as many planes as human life and human association. The men with whom we play golf and tennis, billiards and whist, are friends on the lowest plane—that of common pleasures. Our professional and business associates are friends upon a little higher plane—that of the interests we share. The men who have the same social customs and intellectual tastes; the men with whom we read our favourite authors, and talk over our favourite topics, are friends upon a still higher plane—that of identity of æsthetic and intellectual pursuits. The highest plane, the best friends, are those with whom we consciously share the spiritual purpose of our lives. This highest friendship is as precious as it is rare. With such friends we drop at once into a matter-of-course intimacy and communion. Nothing is held back, nothing is concealed; our aims are expressed with the assurance of sympathy; even our shortcomings are confessed with the certainty that they will be forgiven. Such friendship lasts as long as the virtue which is its common bond. Jealousy cannot come in to break it up. Absolute sincerity, absolute loyalty,— these are the high terms on which such friendship must be held. A person may have many such friends on one condition: that he shall not talk to any one friend about what his friendship permits him to know of another friend. Each such relation must be complete within itself; and hermetically sealed, so far as permitting any one else to come inside the sacred circle of its mutual confidence. In such friendship, differences, as of age, sex, station in life, divide not, but rather enhance, the sweetness and tenderness of the relationship. In Aristotle's words: "The friendship of the good, and of those who have the same virtues, is perfect friendship. Such friendship, therefore, endures so long as each retains his character, and virtue is a lasting thing."

VIII: CRITICISM AND SUMMARY OF ARISTOTLE'S TEACHING

If finally we ask what are the limitations of Aristotle, we find none save the limitations of the age and city in which he lived. He lived in a city-state where thirty thousand full male citizens, with some seventy thousand women and children dependent upon them, were supported by the labour of some hundred thousand slaves. The rights of man as such, whether native or alien, male or female, free or slave, had not yet been affirmed. That crowning proclamation of universal emancipation was reserved for Christianity three centuries and a half later. Without this Christian element no principle of personality is complete. Not until the city-state of Plato and Aristotle is widened to include the humblest man, the lowliest woman, the most defenceless little child, does their doctrine become final and universal. Yet with this single limitation of its range, the form of Aristotle's teaching is complete and ultimate. Deeper, saner, stronger, wiser statement of the principles of personality the world has never heard.

His teaching may be summed up in the following:—

TEN ARISTOTELIAN COMMANDMENTS

Thou shalt devote thy utmost powers to some section of our common social welfare.

Thou shalt hold this end above all lesser goods, such as pleasure, money, honour.

Thou shalt hold the instruments essential to the service of this end second only to the end itself.

Thou shalt ponder and revere the universal laws that bind ends and means together in the ordered universe.

Thou shalt master and obey the specific laws that govern the relation of means to thy chosen end.

Thou shalt use just so much of the materials and tools of life as the service of thy end requires.

Thou shalt exclude from thy life all that exceeds or falls below this mean, reckless of pleasure lost.

Thou shalt endure whatever hardship and privation the maintenance of this mean in the service of thy end requires, heedless of pain involved.

Thou shalt remain steadfast in this service until habit shall have made it a second nature, and custom shall have transformed it into joy.

Thou shalt find and hold a few like-minded friends, to share with thee this lifelong devotion to that common social welfare which is the task and goal of man.

Strato of Lampsacus by Diogenes Laërtius

Theophrastus was succeeded in the presidency of his [the Peripatetic] school by Strato of Lampsacus, the son of Arcesilaus, of whom he had made mention in his will.

He was a man of great eminence, known as 'The Natural Philosopher,' from his surpassing all men in the diligence with which he applied himself to the investigation of matters of that nature.

He was also the preceptor of Ptolemy Philadelphus, and received from him, as it is said, eighty talents; and he began to preside over the school, as Apollodorus tells us in his *Chronicles*, in the hundred and twenty-third Olympiad, and continued in that post for eighteen years.

There are extant three books of his on Kingly Power; three on Justice; three on the Gods; three on Beginnings; and one on each of the subjects of Happiness, Philosophy, Manly Courage, the Vacuum, Heaven, Spirit. Human Nature, the Generation of Animals, Mixtures, Sleep, Dreams, Sight, Perception, Pleasure, Colours, Diseases, Judgments, Powers, Metallic Works, Hunger, and Dimness of Sight, Lightness and Heaviness, Enthusiasm, Pain, Nourishment and Growth, Animals whose Existence is Doubted, Fabulous Animals, Causes, a Solution of Doubts, a preface to Topics; there are, also, treatises on Contingencies, on the Definition, on the More and Less, on Injustice, on Former and Later, on the Prior Genus, on Property, on the Future.

There are, also, two books called the Examination of Inventions; the Genuineness of the Commentaries attributed to him, is doubted.

There is a volume of Epistles, which begins thus: "Strato wishes Arsinoe prosperity."

They say that he became so thin and weak, that he died without its being perceived. And there is an epigram of ours upon him in the following terms:

The man was thin, believe me, from the use
Of frequent unguents; Strato was his name,
A citizen of Lampsacus; he struggled long
With fell disease, and died at last unnoticed.

There were eight people of the name of Strato. The first was a pupil of Isocrates; the second was the man of whom we have been speaking; the third was a physician, a pupil of Erasistratus, or, as some assert, a foster-child of his; the fourth was an historian, who wrote a history of the Achievements of Philip and Perses in their wars against the Romans The sixth was an epigrammatic poet; the seventh was an ancient physician, as Aristotle tells us; the eighth was a Peripatetic philosopher, who lived in Alexandria.

But to return to Strato the physicist whose will is extant, and it is couched in the following language:

"If anything happens to me, I make this disposition of my property. I leave all my property in my house to Lampyrio and Arcesilaus; and with the money which I have at Athens, in the first place, let my executors provide for my funeral and for all other customary expenses; without doing anything extravagant, or, on the other hand, anything mean. And the following shall be my executors, according to this my will: Olympichus, Aristides, Innesigenes, Hippocrates, Epicrates, Gorgylus, Diocles, Lycon, and Athanes, And my school I leave to Lycon, since of the others some are too old, and others too busy. And the rest will do well, if they ratify this arrangement of mine. I also bequeath to him all my books, except such as we have written ourselves; and all my furniture in the dining-room, and the couches, and the drinking cups. And let my executors give Epicrates five hundred drachmas, and one of my slaves, according to the choice made by Arcesilaus. And first of all, let Lampyrion and Arcesilaus cancel the engagements which Daippus has entered into for Iraeus. And let him be acquitted of all obligation to Lampyrion or the heirs of Lampyrion; and let him also be discharged from any bond or note of hand he may have given. And let my executors give him five hundred drachmas of silver, and one of my slaves, whichever Arcesilaus may approve, in order that, as he has done me great service, and co-operated with me in many things, he may have a competency, and be enabled to live decently. And I give their freedom to Diophantus, and Diocles, and Abus. Simias I give to Arcesilaus.

I also give his freedom to Dromo. And when Arcesilaus arrives, let Iraeus calculate with Olympicus and Epicrates, and the rest of my executors, the amount that has been expended on my funeral and on other customary expenses. And let the money that remains, be paid over to Arcesilaus by Olympichus, who shall give him no trouble, as to the time or manner of payment. And Arcesilaus shall discharge the engagements which Strato has entered into with Olympichus and Ausinias, which are preserved in writing in the care of Philoreatos, the son of Tisamenus. And with respect to my monument, let them do whatever seems good to Arcesilaus, and Olympichus, and Lycon.

This is his will, which is still extant, as Aristo the Chian, has collected and published it.

And this Strato was a man, as has been shown above, of deservedly great popularity; having devoted himself to the study of every kind of philosophy, and especially of that branch of it called natural philosophy, which is one of the most ancient and important branches of the whole.

Life of Aristotle by George Grote

In my preceding work, *Plato and the Other Companions of Sokrates*, I described a band of philosophers differing much from each other, but all emanating from Sokrates as common intellectual progenitor; all manifesting themselves wholly or principally in the composition of dialogues; and all living in an atmosphere of Hellenic freedom, as yet untroubled by any overruling imperial ascendancy from without. From that band, among whom Plato is facile princeps, I now proceed to another, among whom the like preeminence belongs to Aristotle. This second band knew the Sokratic stimulus only as an historical tradition; they gradually passed, first from the Sokratic or Platonic dialogue dramatic, colloquial, cross-examining to the Aristotelian dialogue, semi-dramatic, rhetorical, counter-expository; and next to formal theorizing, ingenious solution and divination of special problems, historical criticism and abundant collections of detailed facts: moreover, they were witnesses of the extinction of freedom in Hellas, and of the rise of the Macedonian kingdom out of comparative nullity to the highest pinnacle of supremacy and mastership. Under the successors of Alexander, this extraneous supremacy, intermeddling and dictatorial, not only overruled the political movements of the Greeks, but also influenced powerfully the position and working of their philosophers; and would have become at once equally intermeddling even earlier, under Alexander himself, had not his whole time and personal energy been absorbed by insatiable thirst for eastern conquest, ending with an untimely death.

Aristotle was born at Stageira, an unimportant Hellenic colony in Thrace, which has obtained a lasting name in history from the fact of being his birthplace. It was situated in the Strymonic Gulf, a little north of the isthmus which terminates in the mountainous promontory of Athos; its founders were Greeks from the island of Andros, reinforced afterwards by additional immigrants from Chalkis in Euba. It was, like other Grecian cities, autonomous a distinct, self-governing community; but it afterwards became incorporated in the confederacy of free cities under the presidency of Olynthus. The most material feature in its condition, at the period of Aristotles birth, was, that it lay near the frontier of Macedonia, and not far even from Pella, the residence of the Macedonian king Amyntas (father of Philip). Aristotle was born, not earlier than 392 B.C., nor later than 385-384 B.C. His father, Nikomachus, was a citizen of Stageira, distinguished as a physician, author of some medical works, and boasting of being descended from the heroic gens of the Asklepiads; his mother, Phaestis, was also of good civic family, descended from one of the first Chalkidian colonists. Moreover, Nikomachus was not merely learned in his art, but was accepted as confidential physician and friend of Amyntas, with whom he passed much of his time a circumstance of great moment to the future career of his son. We are told that among the Asklepiads the habit of physical observation, and even manual training in dissection, were imparted traditionally from father to son, from the earliest years, thus serving as preparation for medical practice when there were no written treatises to study. The mind of Aristotle may thus have acquired that appetite for physiological study which so many of his treatises indicate.

Respecting the character of his youth, there existed, even in antiquity, different accounts. We learn that he lost his father and mother while yet a youth, and that he came under the guardianship of Proxenus, a native of Atarneus who had settled at Stageira. According to one account, adopted apparently by the earliest witnesses preserved to us, he was at first an extravagant youth, spent much of his paternal property, and then engaged himself to military service; of which he soon became weary, and went back to Stageira, turning to account the surgical building, apparatus, and medicines left by his father as a medical practitioner. After some time, we know not how long, he retired from this profession, shut up the building, and devoted himself to rhetoric and philosophy. He then went to Athens, and there entered himself in the school of Plato, at the age of thirty. The philosophical life was thus (if this account be believed) a second choice, adopted comparatively late in life. The other account, depending also upon good witnesses, represents him as having come to Athens and enlisted as pupil of Plato, at the early age of seventeen or eighteen: it omits all mention of an antecedent period, occupied by military service and a tentative of medical profession. In both the two narratives, Aristotle appears as resident at Athens, and devoting himself to rhetoric and philosophy, from some period before 360 B.C. down to the death of Plato in 347 B.C.; though, according to the first of the two narratives, he begins his philosophical career at a later age, while his whole life occupied seventy years instead of sixty-two years.

During the interval, 367-360 B.C., Plato was much absent from Athens, having paid two separate visits to Dionysius the younger at Syracuse. The time which he spent there at each visit is not explicitly given; but as far as we can conjecture from indirect allusions, it cannot have been less than a year at each, and may possibly have been longer. If, therefore, Aristotle reached Athens in 367 B.C. (as Hermippus represents) he cannot have enjoyed continuous instructions from Plato for the three or four years next ensuing.

However the facts may stand as to Aristotles early life, there is no doubt that in or before the year 362 B.C. he became resident at Athens, and that he remained there, profiting by the society and lectures of Plato, until the death of the latter in 347 B.C. Shortly after the loss of his master, he quitted Athens, along with his fellow-pupil Xenokrates, and went to Atarneus, which was at that time ruled by the despot Hermeias. That despot was a remarkable man, who being a eunuch through bodily hurt when a child, and having become slave of a prior despot named Eubulus, had contrived to succeed him in the supreme power, and governed the towns of Atarneus and Assos with firmness and energy. Hermeias had been at Athens, had heard Platos lectures, and had contracted friendship with Aristotle; which friendship became farther cemented by the marriage of Aristotle, during his residence at Atarneus, with Pythias the niece of Hermeias. For three years Aristotle and Xenokrates remained at Assos or Atarneus, whence they were then forced to escape by reason of the despots death; for Mentor the Rhodian, general of the Persians in those regions, decoyed Hermeias out of the town under pretence of a diplomatic negotiation, then perfidiously seized him, and sent him up as prisoner to the Persian king, by whose order he was hanged. Mentor at the same time seized the two towns and other possessions of Hermeias, while Aristotle with his wife retired to Mitylene. His deep grief for the fate of Hermeias was testified in a noble hymn or paean which he composed, and which still remains, as well as by an epigram inscribed on the statue of Hermeias at Delphi. We do not hear of his going elsewhere, until, two or three years afterwards (the exact date is differently reported), he was invited by Philip into Macedonia, to become preceptor to the young prince Alexander, then thirteen or fourteen years old. The reputation, which Aristotle himself had by this time established, doubtless coincided with the recollection of his father Nikomachus as physician and friend of Amyntas, in determining Philip to such a choice. Aristotle performed the duties required from him, enjoying the confidence and favour both of Philip and Alexander, until the assassination of the former and the accession of the latter in 336 B.C. His principle residence during this period was in Macedonia, but he paid occasional visits to Athens, and allusion is made to certain diplomatic services which he rendered to the Athenians at the court of Philip; moreover he must have spent some time at his native city Stageira, which had been among the many Greek cities captured and ruined by Philip during the Olynthian war of 349-347 B.C. Having obtained the consent and authority of Philip, Aristotle repaired to Stageira for the purpose of directing the re-establishment of the city. Recalling such of its dispersed inhabitants as could be collected, either out of the neighbouring villages or from more distant parts, he is said to have drawn up laws, or framed regulations for the returned citizens, and new comers. He had reason to complain of various rivals who intrigued against him, gave him much trouble, and obstructed the complete renovation of the city; but, notwithstanding, his services were such that an annual festival was instituted to commemorate them. It is farther stated, that at some time during this period he had a school (analogous to the Academy at Athens) in the Nymphćum of the place called Mieza; where stone seats and shady walks, ennobled by the name of Aristotle, were still shown even in the days of Plutarch.

In 336 B.C. Alexander became king of Macedonia, and his vast projects for conquest, first of Persia, next of other peoples known and unknown, left him no leisure for anything but military and imperial occupations. It was in the ensuing year (335 B.C. when the preparations for the Persian expedition were being completed, ready for its execution in the following spring, that Aristotle transferred his residence to Athens. The Platonic philosophical school in which he had studied was now conducted by Xenokrates as Scholarch, having passed at the death of Plato, in 347 B.C., to his nephew Speusippus, and from the latter to Xenokrates in 339 B.C. Aristotle established for himself a new and rival school on the eastern side of Athens, in the gymnasium attached to the temple of Apollo Lykeius, and deriving from thence the name by which it was commonly known the Lykeium. In that school, and in the garden adjoining, he continued to lecture or teach, during the succeeding twelve years, comprising the life and the brilliant conquests of Alexander. Much of his instruction is said to have been given while walking in the garden, from whence the students and the sect derived the title of Peripatetics. In the business of his school and the composition of his works all his time was occupied; and his scholars soon became so numerous that he found it convenient to desire them to elect from themselves every ten days a rector to maintain order, as Xenokrates had already done at the Academy. Aristotle farther maintained correspondence, not merely with Alexander and Antipater but also with Themison, one of the princes of Cyprus, as Isokrates had corresponded with Nikokles, and Plato with Dionysius of Syracuse.

In June, 323 B.C., occurred the premature and unexpected decease of the great Macedonian conqueror, aged 32 years and 8 months, by a violent fever at Babylon. So vast was his power, and so unmeasured his ambition, that the sudden removal of such a man operated as a shock to the hopes and fears of almost every one, both in Greece and Asia. It produced an entire change in the position of Aristotle at Athens.

To understand what that position really was, we must look at it in connection with his Macedonian sympathies, and with the contemporaneous political sentiment at Athens. It was in the middle of the year 335 B.C., that Alexander put down by force the revolt of the Thebans, took their city by assault, demolished it altogether (leaving nothing but the citadel called Kadmeia, occupied by a Macedonian garrison), and divided its territory between two other Botian towns. Immediately after that terror-striking act, he demanded from the Athenians (who had sympathized warmly with Thebes, though without overt acts of assistance) the surrender of their principal anti-Macedonian politicians. That demand having been refused, he at first prepared to extort compliance at the point of the sword, but was persuaded not without difficulty, to renounce such intention, and to be content with the voluntary exile of Ephialtes and Charidemus from Athens. Though the unanimous vote of the Grecian Synod at Corinth constituted him Imperator, there can be no doubt that the prevalent sentiment in Greece towards him was that of fear and dislike; especially among the Athenians, whose dignity was most deeply mortified, and to whom the restriction of free speech was the most painful.

Now it was just at this moment (in 335 B.C.) that Aristotle came to Athens and opened his school. We cannot doubt that he was already known and esteemed as the author of various published writings. But the prominent mark by which every one now distinguished him, was, that he had been for several years confidential preceptor of Alexander, and was still more or less consulted by that prince, as well as sustained by the friendship of Antipater, viceroy of Macedonia during the kings absence. Aristotle was regarded as philo-Macedonian, and to a certain extent, anti-Hellenic the sentiment expressed towards him in the unfriendly epigram of the contemporary Chian poet Theokritus. His new school, originally opened under the protection and patronage of Alexander and Antipater, continued to be associated with their names, by that large proportion of Athenian citizens who held anti-Macedonian sentiments. Alexander caused the statue of Aristotle to be erected in Athens, and sent to him continual presents of money, usefully employed by the philosopher in the prosecution of his physical and zoological researches, as well as in the purchase of books. Moreover, Aristotle remained in constant and friendly correspondence with Antipater, the resident viceroy at Pella, during the absence of Alexander in Asia. Letters of recommendation from Aristotle to the Macedonian rulers were often given and found useful: several of them were preserved and published afterwards. There is even reason to believe that the son of Antipater Kassander, afterwards viceroy or king of Macedonia, was among his pupils.

I have recounted elsewhere how the character of Alexander became gradually corrupted by unexampled success and Asiatic influences; how he thus came to feel less affection and esteem for Aristotle, to whom he well knew that his newly acquired imperial and semi-divine pretensions were not likely to be acceptable; how, on occasion of the cruel sentence passed on Kallisthenes, he threatened even to punish Aristotle himself, as having recommended Kallisthenes, and as sympathizing with the same free spirit; lastly, how Alexander became more or less alienated, not only from the society of Hellenic citizens, but even from his faithful viceroy, the Macedonian Antipater. But these changed relations between Aristotle and Alexander did not come before the notice of the Athenians, nor alter the point of view in which they regarded the philosopher; the rather, since the relations of Aristotle with Antipater continued as intimate as ever.

It will thus appear, that though all the preserved writings of Aristotle are imbued with a thoroughly independent spirit of theorizing contemplation and lettered industry, uncorrupted by any servility or political bias yet his position during the twelve years between 335-323 B.C. inevitably presented him to the Athenians as the macedonizing philosopher, parallel with Phokion as the macedonizing politician, and in pointed antithesis to Xenokrates at the Academy, who was attached to the democratical constitution, and refused kingly presents. Besides that enmity which he was sure to incur, as an acute and self-thinking philosopher, from theology and the other anti-philosophical veins in the minds of ordinary men, Aristotle thus became the object of unfriendly sentiment from many Athenian patriots, who considered the school of Plato generally as hostile to popular liberty, and who had before their eyes examples of individual Platonists, ruling their respective cities with a sceptre forcibly usurped.

Such sentiment was probably aggravated by the unparalleled and offensive Macedonian demonstration at the Olympic festival of 324 B.C. It was on that occasion that Alexander, about one year prior to his decease, sent down a formal rescript, which was read publicly to the assembled crowd by a herald with loud voice; ordering every Grecian city to recall all exiles who had been banished by judicial sentence, and intimating, that if the rescript were not obeyed spontaneously, Antipater would be instructed to compel the execution of it by force. A large number of the exiles whose restitution was thus ordered, were present on the plain of Olympia, and heard the order proclaimed, doubtless with undisguised triumph and exultation. So much the keener must have been the disgust and humiliation among the other Grecian hearers, who saw the autonomy of each separate city violently trampled down, without even the pretence of enquiry, by this high-handed sentence of the Macedonian conqueror. Among the Athenians especially, the resentment felt was profound; and a vote was passed appointing deputies to visit Alexander in person, for the purpose of remonstrating against it. The orator Demosthenes, who happened to be named Archi-Theôrus of Athens (chief of the solemn legation sent to represent Athens) at this Olympic festival, incurred severe reproach from his accuser Deinarchus, for having even been seen in personal conversation with the Macedonian officer who had arrived from Asia as bearer of this odious rescript.

Now it happened that this officer, the bearer of the rescript, was Nikanor of Stageira; son of Proxenus who had been Aristotles early guardian, and himself the cherished friend or ward, ultimately the son-in-law, of the philosopher. We may be certain that Aristotle would gladly embrace the opportunity of seeing again this attached friend, returning after a long absence on service in Asia; that he would be present with him at the Olympic festival, perhaps receive a visit from him at Athens also. And the unpopularity of Aristotle at Athens, as identified with Macedonian imperial authority, would thus be aggravated by his notorious personal alliance with his fellow-citizen Nikanor, the bearer of that rescript in which such authority had been most odiously manifested.

Nikanor was appointed afterwards (in 318 B.C., five years later than the death of Aristotle) by Kassander, son of Antipater, to be commander of the Macedonian garrison which occupied Munychia, as a controlling force over Athens (Diodor. xviii. 64). It will be seen in my History of Greece (ch. xcvi. p. 458) that Kassander was at that moment playing a difficult game, his father Antipater being just dead; that he could only get possession of Munychia by artifice, and that it was important for him to entrust the mission to an officer who already had connections at Athens; that Nikanor, as adopted son of Aristotle, possessed probably beforehand acquaintance with Phokion and the other macedonizing leaders at Athens; so that the ready way in which Phokion now fell into co-operation with him is the more easily explained.

Nikanor, however, was put to death by Kassander himself, some months afterwards.

During the twelve or thirteen years of Aristotles teaching and Alexanders reign, Athens was administered by macedonizing citizens, with Phokion and Demades at their head. Under such circumstances, the enmity of those who hated the imperial philosopher could not pass into act; nor was it within the contemplation of any one, that only one year after that rescript which insulted the great Pan-Hellenic festival, the illustrious conqueror who issued it would die of fever, in the vigour of his age and at the height of his power (June, 323 B.C.). But as soon as the news of his decease, coming by surprise both on friends and enemies, became confirmed, the suppressed anti-Macedonian sentiment burst forth in powerful tide, not merely at Athens, but also throughout other parts of Greece. There resulted that struggle against Antipater, known as the Lamian war: a gallant struggle, at first promising well, but too soon put down by superior force, and ending in the occupation of Athens by Antipater with a Macedonian garrison in September, 322 B.C., as well as in the extinction of free speech and free citizenship by the suicide of Demosthenes and the execution of Hypereides.

During the year immediately succeeding the death of Alexander, the anti-Macedonian sentiment continued so vehemently preponderant at Athens, that several of the leading citizens, friends of Phokion, left the city to join Antipater, though Phokion himself remained, opposing ineffectually the movement. It was during this period that the enemies of Aristotle found a favourable opportunity for assailing him. An indictment on the score of impiety was preferred against him by Eurymedon the Hierophant (chief priest of the Eleusinian Demeter), aided by Demophilus, son of the historian Ephorus. The Hymn or Paean (still existing), which Aristotle had composed in commemoration of the death, and in praise of the character, of the eunuch Hermeias, was arraigned as a mark of impiety; besides which Aristotle had erected at Delphi a statue of Hermeias with an honorific inscription, and was even alleged to have offered sacrifices to him as to a god. In the published writings of Aristotle, too, the accusers found various heretical doctrines, suitable for sustaining their indictment; as, for example, the declaration that prayer and sacrifices to the gods were of no avail. But there can be little doubt that the Hymn, Ode, or Paean, in honour of Hermeias, would be more offensive to the feelings of an ordinary Athenian than any philosophical dogma extracted from the cautious prose compositions of Aristotle. It is a hymn, of noble thought and dignified measure, addressed to Virtue, in which are extolled the semi-divine or heroic persons who had fought, endured, and perished in her service. The name and exploits of Hermeias are here introduced as the closing parallel and example in a list beginning with Heraklęs, the Dioskűri, Achilles, and Ajax. Now the poet Kallistratus, in his memorable Skolion, offers a like compliment to Harmodius and Aristogeiton; and Pindar, to several free Greeks of noble family, who paid highly for his epinician Odes now remaining. But all the persons thus complimented were such as had gained prizes at the sacred festivals, or had distinguished themselves in other ways which the public were predisposed to honour; whereas Hermeias was a eunuch, who began by being a slave, and ended by becoming despot over a free Grecian community, without any exploit conspicuous to the eye. To many of the Athenian public it would seem insult, and even impiety, to couple Hermeias with the greatest personages of Hellenic mythology, as a successful competitor for heroic honours. We need only read the invective of Claudian against Eutropius, to appreciate the incredible bitterness of indignation and contempt, which was suggested by the spectacle of a eunuch and a slave exercising high public functions. And the character of a despot was, to the anti-macedonizing Athenians, hardly less odious than either of the others combined with it in Hermeias.

Among the titles of the lost works of Aristotle, one is Περὶ Εὐχῆς. From its position in the Catalogue, it seems plainly to have been a dialogue; and the dialogues were the most popular and best-known writings of Aristotle. Now we know from the Nikomach. Ethica that Aristotle declared all constructive effort, and all action with a view to external ends, to be inconsistent with the Divine Nature, which was blest exclusively in theorizing and contemplation. If he advocated the same doctrine in the dialogue Περὶ Εὐχῆς, he must have contended that persons praying could have no additional chance of obtaining the benefits which they prayed for; and this would have placed him in conflict with the received opinions.

Taking these particulars into account, we shall see that a charge thus sustained, when preferred by a venerable priest, during the prevalence of strong anti-Macedonian feeling, against a notorious friend of Antipater and Nikanor, was quite sufficient to alarm the prudence of the accused. Aristotle bowed to the storm (if indeed he had not already left Athens, along with other philo-Macedonians) and retired to Chalkis (in Euba), then under garrison by Antipater. An accused person at Athens had always the option of leaving the city, at any time before the day of trial; Sokrates might have retired, and obtained personal security in the same manner, if he had chosen to do so. Aristotle must have been served, of course, with due notice: and according to Athenian custom, the indictment would be brought into court in his absence, as if he had been present; various accusers, among them Demochares, the nephew of Demosthenes, would probably speak in support of it; and Aristotle must been found guilty in his absence. But there is no ground for believing that he intended to abandon Athens, and live at Chalkis, permanently; the rather, inasmuch as he seems to have left not only his school, but his library, at Athens under the charge of Theophrastus. Aristotle knew that the Macedonian chiefs would not forego supremacy over Greece without a struggle; and, being in personal correspondence with Antipater himself, he would receive direct assurance of this resolution, if assurance were needed. In a question of military force, Aristotle probably felt satisfied that Macedonian arms must prevail; after which the affairs of Athens would be again administered, at least in the same spirit, as they had been before Alexanders death, if not with more complete servility. He would then have returned thither to resume his school, in competition with that of Plato under Xenokrates at the Academy; for he must have been well aware that the reputation of Athens, as central hearth of Hellenic letters and philosophy, could not be transferred to Chalkis or to any other city.

We do not know upon what foundation of fact (if upon any) these allegations were advanced by a contemporary orator. But they are curious, as illustrating the view taken of Aristotle by his enemies. They must have been delivered as parts of one of the accusatory speeches on Aristotles trial par contumace: for this was the earliest occasion on which Aristotles enemies had the opportunity of publicly proclaiming their antipathy against him, and they would hardly omit to avail themselves of it. The Hierophant, the principal accuser, would be supported by other speakers following him; just as Meletus, the accuser of Sokrates, was supported by Anytus and Lykon. The ἱστορίαι of Demochares were not composed until seventeen years after this epoch certainly not earlier than 306 B.C. sixteen years after the death of Aristotle, when his character was not prominently before the public. Nevertheless Demochares may possibly have included these accusatory allegations against the philosopher in his ἱστορίαι, as well as in his published speech. His invectives against Antipater, and the friends of Antipater, were numerous and bitter. Philon, who indicted Sophokles for the law which the latter had proposed in 306 B.C. against the philosophers at Athens, had been a friend of Aristotle.

This is what would probably have occurred, when the Lamian war was finished and the Macedonian garrison installed at Athens, in Sept. 322 B.C. had Aristotles life lasted longer. But in or about that very period, a little before the death of Demosthenes, he died at Chalkis of illness; having for some time been troubled with indigestion and weakness of stomach. The assertion of Eumelus and others that he took poison, appears a mere fiction suggested by the analogy of Sokrates. One of his latest compositions was a defence of himself against the charge of impiety, and against the allegations of his accusers (as reported to him, or published) in support of it. A sentence of this defence remains, wherein he points out the inconsistency of his accusers in affirming that he intended to honour Hermeias as an immortal, while he had notoriously erected a tomb, and had celebrated funeral ceremonies to him as a mortal. And in a letter to Antipater, he said (among other things) that Athens was a desirable residence, but that the prevalence of sycophancy or false accusation was a sad drawback to its value; moreover that he had retired to Chalkis, in order that the Athenians might not have the opportunity of sinning a second time against philosophy, as they had already done once, in the person of Sokrates. In the same or another letter to Antipater, he adverted to an honorific tribute which had been voted to him at Delphi before the death of Alexander, but the vote for which had been since rescinded. He intimated that this disappointment was not indifferent to him, yet at the same time no serious annoyance.

We learn from Diogenes that Theophrastus was indicted for impiety by Agnonides; but such was the esteem in which Theophrastus was held, that the indictment utterly failed; and Agnonides was very near incurring the fine which every accuser had to pay, if he did not obtain one-fifth of the suffrages of the Dikasts (Diog. L. v. 37). Now Agnonides comes forward principal-principally as the vehement accuser of Phokion four years after the death of Aristotle, during the few months of democratical reaction brought about by the edicts and interference of Polysperchon (318 B.C.) after the death of Antipater (History of Greece, ch. xcvi. p. 477). Agnonides must have felt himself encouraged by what had happened five years before with Aristotle, to think that he would succeed in a similar charge against Theophrastus. But Theophrastus was personally esteemed; he was not intimately allied with Antipater, or directly protected by him; moreover, he had composed no hymn to a person like Hermeias. Accordingly, the indictment recoiled upon the accuser himself.

In regard to the person and habits of Aristotle, we are informed that he had thin legs and small eyes; that in speech he was somewhat lisping; that his attire was elegant and even showy; that his table was well-served according to his enemies, luxurious above the measure of philosophy. His pleasing and persuasive manners are especially attested by Antipater, in a letter, apparently of marked sympathy and esteem, written shortly after the philosophers death. He was deeply attached to his wife Pythias, by whom he had a daughter who bore the same name. His wife having died after some years, he then re-married with a woman of Stageira, named Herpyllis, who bore him a son called Nikomachus. Herpyllis lived with him until his death; and the constant as well as reciprocal attachment between them is attested by his last will. At the time of his death, his daughter Pythias had not yet attained marriageable age; Nikomachus was probably a child.

The will or testament of the philosopher is preserved. Its first words constitute Antipater his general executor in the most comprehensive terms, words well calculated to ensure that his directions should be really carried into effect; since not only was Antipater now the supreme potentate, but Nikanor, the chief beneficiary under the will, was in his service and dependent on his orders. Aristotle then proceeds to declare that Nikanor shall become his son-in-law, by marriage with his daughter Pythias as soon as she shall attain suitable age; also, his general heir, subject to certain particular bequests and directions, and the guardian of his infant son Nikomachus. Nikanor being at that time on service, and perhaps in Asia, Aristotle directs that four friends shall take provisional care of Herpyllis, his two children, and his effects, until Nikanor can appear and act: Theophrastus is to be conjoined with these four if he chooses, and if circumstances permit him. The daughter Pythias, when she attains suitable age, is to become the wife of Nikanor, who will take the best care both of her and her son Nikomachus, being in the joint relation of father and brother to them. If Pythias shall die, either before the marriage or after it, but without leaving offspring, Nikanor shall have discretion to make such arrangements as may be honourable both for himself and for the testator respecting Nikomachus and the estate generally. In case of the death of Nikanor himself, either before the marriage or without offspring, any directions given by him shall be observed; but Theophrastus shall be entitled, if he chooses, to become the husband of Pythias, and if Theophrastus does not choose, then the executors along with Antipater shall determine what they think best both for her and for Nikomachus. The will then proceeds as follows: The executors (here Antipater is not called in to co-operate) with Nikanor, in faithful memory of me and of the steady affection of Herpyllis towards me, shall take good care of her in every way, but especially if she desires to be married, in giving her away to one not unworthy of me. They shall assign to her, besides what she has already received, a talent of silver, and three female slaves chosen by herself, out of the property, together with the young girl and the Pyrrhean slave now attached to her person. If she prefers to reside at Chalkis, she may occupy the lodging near the garden; if at Stageira, she may live at my paternal house. Whichever of the two she may prefer, the executors shall provide it with all such articles of furniture as they deem sufficient for her comfort and dignity.

We find in the will of Theophrastus (Diog. L. v. 52) mention made of a property (χωρίον) at Stageira belonging to Theophrastus, which he bequeaths to Kallinus. Probably this is the same property which had once belonged to Aristotle; for I do not see how else Theophrastus (who was a native of Eresus in Lesbos) could have become possessed of property at Stageira.

Aristotle proceeds to direct that Nikanor shall make comfortable provision for several persons mentioned by name, male and female, most of them slaves, but one (Myrmex), seemingly, a free boarder or pupil, whose property he had undertaken to manage. Two or three of these slaves are ordered to be liberated, and to receive presents, as soon as his daughter Pythias shall be married. He strictly enjoins that not one of the youthful slaves who attended him shall be sold. They are to be brought up and kept in employment; when of mature age, they are to be liberated according as they shew themselves worthy.

Aristotle had in his lifetime ordered, from a sculptor named Gryllion, busts of Nikanor and of the mother of Nikanor; he intended farther to order from the same sculptor a bust of Proxenus, Nikanors father. Nikanor is instructed by the will to complete these orders, and to dedicate the busts properly when brought in. A bust of the mother of Aristotle is to be dedicated to Demeter at Nemea, or in any other place which Nikanor may prefer; another bust of Arimnęstus (brother of Aristotle) is to be dedicated as a memento of the same, since he has died childless.

During some past danger of Nikanor (we do not know what) Aristotle had made a vow of four marble animal figures, in case the danger were averted, to Zeus the Preserver and Athęnę the Preserver. Nikanor is directed to fulfil this vow and to dedicate the figures in Stageira.

Here is a vow, made by Aristotle to the gods under some unknown previous emergency, which he orders his executor to fulfil. I presume that the last words of direction given by Sokrates before his death to Kriton were of the same nature: We owe a cock to Asculapius: pay the debt, and do not fail.

Lastly, wherever Aristotle is buried, the bones of his deceased wife Pythias are to be collected and brought to the same spot, as she had commanded during her lifetime.

This testament is interesting, as it illustrates the personal circumstances and sentiments of the philosopher, evincing an affectionate forethought and solicitude for those who were in domestic relations with him. As far as we can judge, the establishment and property which he left must have been an ample one. How the provisions of the will were executed, or what became of most persons named in it, we do not know, except that Pythias the daughter of Aristotle was married three times: first, to Nikanor (according to the will); secondly, to Proklęs, descendant of Demaratus (the king of Sparta formerly banished to Asia) by whom she had two sons, Proklęs and Demaratus, afterwards pupils in the school of Theophrastus; thirdly, to a physician named Metrodôrus, by whom she had a son named Aristotle.

Respecting this younger Aristotle son of Metrodorus and grandson of the great philosopher mention is made in the testament of Theophrastus, and directions are given for promoting his improvement in philosophy. Nikomachus was brought up chiefly by Theophrastus, but perished young in battle.

There existed in antiquity several works, partly by contemporaries like the Megaric Eubulides, partly by subsequent Platonists, in which Aristotle was reproached with ingratitude to Plato, servility to the Macedonian power, love of costly display and indulgences, &c. What proportion of truth may lie at the bottom of these charges we do not know enough to determine confidently; but we know that he had many enemies, philosophical as well as political; and controversy on those grounds (then as now) was rarely kept free from personal slander and invective.

The accusation of ingratitude or unbecoming behaviour to Plato is no way proved by any evidence now remaining. It seems to have been suggested to the Platonists mainly, if not wholly, by the direct rivalry of Aristotle in setting up a second philosophical school at Athens, alongside of the Academy; by his independent, self-working, philosophical speculation; and by the often-repeated opposition which he made to some capital doctrines of Plato, especially to the so-called Platonic Ideas. Such opposition was indeed expressed, as far as we can judge, in terms of respectful courtesy, and sometimes even of affectionate regret; examples of which we shall have to notice in going through the Aristotelian writings. Yet some Platonists seem to have thought that direct attack on the masters doctrines was undutiful and ungrateful in the pupil, however unexceptionable the language might be. They also thought, probably, that the critic misrepresented what he sought to refute. Whether Aristotle really believed that he had superior claims to be made Scholarch of the Platonic school at the death of Plato in 347 B.C., or at the death of Speusippus in 339 B.C., is a point which we can neither affirm nor deny. But we can easily understand that the act of setting up a new philosophical school at Athens, though perfectly fair and admissible on his part, was a hostile competition sure both to damage and offend the pre-established school, and likely enough to be resented with unbecoming asperity. Ingratitude towards the great common master Plato, with arrogant claims of superiority over fellow-pupils, were the allegations which this resentment would suggest, and which many Platonists in the Academy would not scruple to advance against their macedonizing rival at the Lykeium.

Such allegations moreover would find easy credence from other men of letters, whose enmity Aristotle had incurred, and to a certain extent even provoked Isokrates and his numerous disciples.

This celebrated rhetor was an elderly man at the zenith of his glory and influence, during those earlier years which Aristotle passed at Athens before the decease of Plato. The Isokratean school was then the first in Greece, frequented by the most promising pupils from cities near and far, perhaps even by Aristotle himself. The political views and handling, as well as the rhetorical style of which the master set the example, found many imitators. Illustrious statesmen, speakers, and writers traced their improvement to this teaching. So many of the pupils, indeed, acquired celebrity among them Theodektęs, Theopompus, Ephorus, Naukrates, Philiskus, Kephisodôrus, and others that Hermippus thought it worth his while to draw up a catalogue of them: many must have been persons of opulent family, highly valuing the benefit received from Isokrates, since each of them was required to pay to him a fee of 1000 drachma. During the first sojourn of Aristotle in Athens (362-347 B.C.), while he was still attached to and receiving instruction from Plato, he appears to have devoted himself more to rhetoric than to philosophy, and even to have given public lessons or lectures on rhetoric. He thus entered into rivalry with Isokrates, for whom, as a teacher and author, he contracted dislike or contempt.

The composition of Isokrates was extremely elegant: his structure of sentences was elaborate even to excess, his arrangement of words rhythmical, his phrases nicely balanced in antithetical equipoise, like those of his master Gorgias; the recital of his discourses proved highly captivating to the ear. Moreover, he had composed a book of rhetorical precepts known and esteemed by Cicero and Quintilian. Besides such technical excellence, Isokrates strove to attain, and to a certain extent actually attained, a higher order of merit. He familiarized his pupils with thoughts and arguments of lofty bearing and comprehensive interest; not assisting them to gain victory either in any real issue tried before the Dikasts, or in any express motion about to be voted on by the public assembly, but predisposing their minds to prize above all things the great Pan-hellenic aggregate its independence in regard to external force, and internal harmony among its constituent cities, with a reasonable recognition of presidential authority, equitably divided between Athens and Sparta, and exercised with moderation by both. He inculcated sober habits and deference to legal authority on the part of the democrats of Athens; he impressed upon princes, like Philip and Nikokles, the importance of just and mild bearing towards subjects. Such is the general strain of the discourses which we now possess from Isokrates; though he appears to have adopted it only in middle life, having begun at first in the more usual track of the logographer composing speeches to be delivered before the Dikastery by actual plaintiffs or defendants, and acquiring thus both reputation and profit. His reputation as a teacher was not only maintained but even increased when he altered his style; and he made himself peculiarly attractive to foreign pupils who desired to acquire a command of graceful expressions, without special reference to the Athenian Assembly and Dikastery. But his new style being midway between Demosthenes and Plato between the practical advocate and politician on one side, and the generalizing or speculative philosopher on the other he incurred as a semi-philosopher, professing to have discovered the juste milieu, more or less of disparagement from both extremes; and Aristotle, while yet a young man in the Platonic school, raised an ardent controversy against his works, on the ground both of composition and teaching. Though the whole controversy is now lost, there is good ground for believing that Aristotle must have displayed no small acrimony. He appears to have impugned the Isokratean discourses, partly as containing improper dogmas, partly as specimens of mere unimpressive elegance, intended for show, pomp, and immediate admiration from the hearer ad implendas aures but destitute both of comprehensive theory and of applicability to any useful purpose. Kephisodôrus, an intimate friend and pupil of Isokrates, defended him in an express reply, attacking both Aristotle the scholar and Plato the master. This reply was in four books, and Dionysius characterizes it by an epithet of the highest praise.

These polemics of Aristotle were begun during his first residence at Athens, prior to 347 B.C., the year of Platos decease, and at the time when he was still accounted a member of the Platonic school. They exemplify the rivalry between that school and the Isokratean, which were then the two competing places of education at Athens: and we learn that Aristotle, at that time only a half-fledged Platonist, opened on his own account not a new philosophical school in competition with Plato, as some state, but a new rhetorical school in opposition to Isokrates. But the case was different at the latter epoch, 335 B.C., when Aristotle came to reside at Athens for the second time. Isokrates was then dead, leaving no successor, so that his rhetorical school expired with him. Aristotle preferred philosophy to rhetoric: he was no longer trammelled by the living presence and authority of Plato. The Platonic school at the Academy stood at that time alone, under Xenokrates, who, though an earnest and dignified philosopher, was deficient in grace and in persuasiveness, and had been criticized for this defect even by Plato himself. Aristotle possessed those gifts in large measure, as we know from the testimony of Antipater. By these circumstances, coupled with his own established reputation and well-grounded self-esteem, he was encouraged to commence a new philosophical school; a school, in which philosophy formed the express subject of the morning lecture, while rhetoric was included as one among the subjects of more varied and popular instruction given in the afternoon. During the twelve ensuing years, Aristotles rivalry was mainly against the Platonists or Xenokrateans at the Academy; embittered on both sides by acrimonious feelings, which these expressed by complaining of his ingratitude and unfairness towards the common master, Plato.

There were thus, at Athens, three distinct parties inspired with unfriendly sentiment towards Aristotle: first, the Isokrateans; afterwards, the Platonists; along with both, the anti-Macedonian politicians. Hence we can account for what Themistius entitles the army of assailants (στράτον ὅλον) that fastened upon him, for the unfavourable colouring with which his domestic circumstances are presented, and for the necessity under which he lay of Macedonian protection; so that when such protection was nullified, giving place to a reactionary fervour, his residence at Athens became both disagreeable and insecure.

Theophrastus by George Malcolm Stratton

In the fragments which have come to us of his account of vision Theophrastus seems to have held with Aristotle that light is not itself a body, or a corpuscular emanation. If we are to regard darkness as something visible,—although at this point he leaves it an open question whether it is a visible object,—then light is not the universal and indispensable condition of sight. He does not doubt, however, that light is visible.

And again the transparent, like light, is not a body, but rather a condition or effect produced in a body—in air, water, aether, and certain solid bodies. Yet instead of regarding light as the actuality of the transparent, as Aristotle had done, Theophrastus entertains the thought that the relation might be reversed, and the transparent be called the actuality of light. But after all, he sagely adds, we need not trouble ourselves about the mere words; it is more important to understand the character of the facts themselves.

Colour, for Theophrastus, is the cause of our seeing colours. He rejects Plato's idea that colour is a flame; there is, he admits, a certain resemblance between white and flame, but black would seem to be flame's very opposite. A simple colour does not differ from another simple colour merely in quantity; we can mix them in equal quantities, and take an equal 'number', say, of the white and of the black. There is, then, a difference between black and white which we must recognize as qualitative.

As for a decision how many 'simple' colours there are, we know that he recognized the difficulty of determining what colours are simple and what compound. Black and white had traditionally been regarded as the only primary colours, and from these all others had been thought to be derived; and the attempt on the part of Democritus to assume a larger number of primaries is viewed by Theophrastus with some suspicion. He himself recognizes seven kinds of colour, or eight if dusky gray is to be distinguished, he says, from black, — although he does not say that these seven or eight colours are all primaries.

Of the particular colours as they occur in nature he has much to say, without making their interrelation clear. White and black he seems to have regarded as alike lacking in light. The air is by its very nature black. And smoke is black because it is composed of moisture dissolved in breath, or air, and earth. These will appear ruddy in so far as they have fire in them;

white seen through black appears crimson, as when the sun is seen through smoke or gloom.

Passing now from the physics of vision to its physiology, we find Theophrastus rejecting the theory that vision is a function of the body as a whole. He also makes a spirited attack on the idea that objects make an imprint on the air, and that this imprint comes to us and causes vision—for air, he holds, is not to be moulded in this way, like wax; indeed water would seem to be better suited to receive such imprints than is the air, yet we see not so well by its means. And farther, he sees great difficulty in the theory that vision is due to the tiny image or reflection in the eye, however this image may be produced. For in the first place the size of the image is not that of the objects seen; in the reflection there cannot be enough contrasting objects at one and the same time to explain the variety of the objects we simultaneously see; and a number of features besides size, which vision detects, e.g., the motion and the distance of objects, are not adequately represented in the ocular image. And moreover many animals that possess sight, have eyes that do not reflect things at all,—animals that have hard and horny eyes, and aquatic animals generally. Finally if reflection explains vision, why does not many a lifeless thing that reflects,—water, for example, and polished bronze—have vision?

As for the positive character of the visual process, Theophrastus has left us much in doubt. He seems to have re-adopted to some extent the idea that in the visual act something issues from the eye—a long-standing idea which Aristotle had rejected. For only in such a way does it seem possible to understand Theophrastus's explanation of the connection between vision and dizziness. We become dizzy in looking down from great heights, he says, because 'vision' (in which he seems to include something extended from the pupil of the eye, in a way familiar to us from Plato) now straining and stretching into the distance, trembles and quivers; and 'vision' thus quivering and set in motion, sets in motion and produces the shape, would seem to soften his scoffing words about 'air prints', when it came to explaining the special visual fact of mirroring

While admitting the role which the water of the eye may play, he is not inclined to ascribe to it exclusively the visual function. Like Plato, and unlike Aristotle, he attributes an important place to the fire within the eye. The exceptional night-vision which some animals possess, he believes is probably due to an intense fire in their eyes, comparable to the inherent glow which certain objects display at night. And from this we may infer that in day-vision also the fire of the eye, but now a weaker fire, was for him an important element, - a thought which seems also to be close to his explanation of the impossibility of gazing at the sun or at anything exceeding bright.

For this is due, he says, to the fact that a stronger light extinguishes a weaker - a relation and effect which elsewhere is asserted of fire; and while he may not have meant that the sun when gazed at extinguished the inherent light, or fire, of the eye, yet in view of his theory of nocturnal vision, just described, such an interpretation would not seem strained. Finally we know that he had little patience with the thought that the size of the eye had any important bearing upon the general keenness of sight. Instead of any general superiority of vision in animals with large eyes, as Anaxagoras had held, Theophrastus questions whether small-eyed animals may not surpass them in visual power; yet in the end he leaves it undecided. On the whole, the composition or constitution of the organ, as of the body generally, he regards as of more importance than its mere size.

The sense of hearing has a certain connection with that of smell, for both of these senses receive from the air their stimulation. But the air is not of itself a sufficient cause of the sensations aroused in smell and hearing; for were this so, we ought to hear odours as well as sounds, and smell sounds as well as odours, and obtain comparable perceptions also from the air in the throat or wind-pipe. The air, if it is to be perceived by hearing or by smell, must have a right relation to the particular sense; and that which gives it a right relation to the organ of hearing is of course different from that which gives it a suitable relation to the sense of smell. In the case of smell there is some peculiar kind of mixture, and the air has suffered some kind of change; while for hearing, the air has been given a special form, or 'figure.' He defends the Aristotelian thesis that sound is connected universally with 'solid' bodies, even though there comes sound from wind and thunder.

He holds that there are tonal differences that cannot be regarded as mere differences of quantity; high tones and low possess some intrinsic distinction which makes it possible for them to bring forth harmony. So far as amount is concerned, a harmonious combination may be of tones that are equal. High and low both have their peculiar character. A shrill tone is not necessarily of greater amount than a deep tone; each may have a like degree and amount of motion, but a motion of different character. The idea of figure, and not of mere amount, must be employed to explain the differences Theophrastus also observes that a ringing in the ears tends to blunt the organ's sensitivity—an observation which he turns against those who urge, as a principle, that like is perceived by like. Change and contrast, and not monotony, have the truly stimulating effect on our sense of hearing. In describing more particularly the bodily process of hearing, he speaks of heat as common to the ear and to the other sense organs. But air is the material more especially composing the organ of hearing—air which elsewhere he describes as 'cut off' and set in motion. There is, therefore, a correspondence of inner and outer in the case of hearing,—the inner air in motion, is the means by which we perceive the motions of the outer air,—a correspondence which Theophrastus recognizes as being exceptional to his general position that perception moves by difference rather than by similarity. With explicit reference to hearing, he rejects the thought that perception is not a local bodily process but is a function of the body as a whole.

Hearing is the sense that most deeply stirs our emotions." Music he regarded as a movement of the soul by which we are freed of the evils that come of passion.

We have seen how Theophrastus makes the air a common factor in the senses of hearing and of smell, while yet asserting that it is no sufficient cause of the sensations aroused in either of these senses. The air must be specially modified, must be given a proper form or schema, before it can affect our hearing; for our sense of smell the air must have undergone a peculiar mixture, it must have suffered some kind of change. Let us now observe further the account he gives of smell.

It is generally agreed, he tells us, that some sort of emanation occurs in odour. Yet he himself finds difficulty in this traditional belief. For any emanation seems necessarily to imply a loss of substance; and were odours to arise by emanation, it would follow that "those substances with the strongest odour would most rapidly perish. Now the fact is nearly the reverse: the most fragrant plants and other bodies that are most odorous are the most enduring." And close to this objection, if not but another phase of it, is his refusal to accept the idea that volatile or light bodies most strongly affect the sense of smell. The mere lightness is not enough: there must be some specific odour present in what is light. "For air and fire are the very lightest of substances, and yet produce in us no sensation of odour."

To this list of the inodorous substances, he elsewhere adds a third, and with it gives an explanation. Water, air, and fire have no odour, he says, because they are simple, and all simple substances, of which these are but examples, are inodorous; whereas earth either is the only substance that has odour or is the substance giving us odour in its most pronounced form, just because earth is the most mixed of substances.

Mixture, then, is essential to odour; and if air, fire, or water seems to possess odour, this is because it is no longer pure. But along with the mixture to account for the odour, and apparently as a process differing from mixture, he speaks of an alteration, an 'alloiosis,' of the substance. No clear outline of this alteration is given us; but in regard to the character of the 'mixture' we are left with somewhat more detail. Odour, he tells us, consists of the dry ingredient in savour, present in what is transparent, for this transparent factor is something common to air and waters. And in speaking more particularly of artificial preparations, he states the different ways in which the moist and the dry may be combined, and the need of intelligent skill to bring about desirable combinations. Yet the odour itself can at times be over-mixed, and will affect our senses more strongly if we can obtain it somewhat simplified. Thus certain flowers,—for example, violets,—are for us more fragrant at a distance because the grosser and more earthy effluvia are left behind.

Theophrastus is less dismayed than were many of his predecessors at the great variety of odours. He will by no means admit the impossibility of finding in them any true differences of kind. Some odours, he grants, are impossible to classify." But on the whole we may hope for success here quite as in the case of savours; for quite as do the savours, the different odours produce in us different organic effects, in addition to their differences in pleasure or unpleasantness, upon which Plato laid such stress.

Fragrance, on the other hand, is the quality in substances that are softened by heat and have become subtile and farthest removed from what is earthy; while the opposites of these are offensive. He recognizes the fact that qualities from more than one class may be present in a single odour, for the 'sweets' may reveal a certain 'sharpness,' and odours may be 'heavy' that on the whole are pleasant. Elsewhere, without saying what the classes are, he is attracted by the idea that they are properly seven, and this he says without suggesting, as he does for colour and for savour, that this number of the classes of odours could easily be enlarged to eight.

Some of the external conditions that influence odour already have appeared. We may add that he finds, on the whole, that dryness is favourable to odour, and especially to the fragrant odours; yet for the time of day and of the year this general rule that heat is a favourable condition must not be pressed too far; for the time of greatest fragrance of flowers is not at midsummer nor in the heat of noon.

Passing now from the character of the stimulus to that of the sensory organ and of the processes that there occur, we find Theophrastus hesitant and in a measure inconsistent as to the connection between smell and breathing. But in any event, the organ of smell is not of some pure and unmixed substance, although air is unquestionably the more prominent or dominant constituent of this organ. Nor does this inner air merely of itself give assurance that the external object which is so closely bound with air will be perceived; as already has been pointed out, there must be some effective ratio between organ and object. And furthermore our sense of smell as well as the external odour is made ineffectual by cold. And certain diseased or otherwise abnormal conditions of the organ may make the sense entirely incapable of sensation; or it may by the presence of one odour be made insensible to some other; or by sheer excess of stimulation be made incapable of perception.

In general the human sense of smell is, we may say, the very worst; for many things that evidently have for animals a characteristic odour are for us inodorous.

There is also this further difference between the sense of smell in man and in animals, that with few or none of the animals is odour sought for its own sake but only incidentally, because it indicates the presence of food; and this, and not the odour itself, is desired; whereas with us, while certain odours are pleasant by such association, others are pleasant independently and of themselves. With animals the closer connection between nutrition and the pleasantness of the odour also explains the noticeable repugnance which certain of them show to odours that to us are most delightful. The idea of opposition to nature, to which allusion already has been made, here is introduced as a conscious principle of explaining the varying responses connected with the sense of smell.

The relation of smell to taste, of which we have here a glimpse, appears as most intimate in all Theophrastus's account. They are not merely neighbouring and mutually helpful senses, inasmuch as savours are aided by the fragrance of what we eat or drink; they are even kindred in many ways. The subjective effect in the two cases shows a close resemblance, although the two processes do not occur in the same parts of the body. The stimuli also are alike in being composite and not simple; they become adapted to our senses by mixture and alteration; and both tastes and odours are often artificially improved by still farther mixing and blending, of which he gives the kinds and character. Stimuli and senses are, in the two cases, similarly affected by cold. Moreover no odour is tasteless, nor is any savour odourless; and in general a change of odour in any substance implies a change of taste. In odours and savours there are common qualities, like sweetness; and there are many designations —though by no means all—common to the classes in the two regions, whose natures really are not far apart.

But while in general the classifications of odour and of savour run parallel, we find no precise and absolute correspondence. In plants the fermentative action by which savour is produced is not precisely the same as that which produces flavour. Savours exist which no one would think of calling odours. Furthermore in spite of the general connection between the odour and the nutritive character of a substance, the pleasures of taste and of smell do not go hand in hand: fragrant things are not always agreeable to the taste, and some things agreeable to taste have an offensive smell.

In what has just preceded, there have appeared many of the features which Theophrastus ascribed to the stimulus and to the physiological process of taste in common with that of smell, and these need not here be repeated. But speaking of taste as distinguished from smell, he says that its external stimulus is a commingling of the dry and the earthy with the moist, or it is a filtration, or infusion, of the dry through the moist under the influence of heat—the two accounts perhaps amounting to the same thing. In all the savours there is a common material, namely moisture; and under the action of heat— either resident or coming from the sun—they change from kind to kind, from opposite into opposite. Yet the different saps or liquids connected with taste have a somewhat different relation to the moist and the dry, though these are present in them all: sour and harsh are closer to the moist; whereas the pungent and the sweet are closer to dryness.

As to the classification of savours, we have from Theophrastus a variety of proposals. He casts doubt on a fourfold classification which he attributes to Plato, nor does he believe that there is an endless number of tastes as was held by Menestor and other ancient scientists. He prefers to be counted with those who hold that the number of tastes is limited, and that what appear as an endless number are derived from these by mixture. At times he seems to entertain the thought of two primary savours, namely bitter and sweet, and of all others as derivatives of these; but without committing himself clearly to such a doctrine. In a certain sense, however, he evidently regards these savours as something like 'principles'. Bitter is the normal taste of all things that are fragrant; it is perhaps a certain form or phase of fragrance itself And sweet is the primal source of all the pleasant savours; under it he names as varieties, the flavour of honey, of wine, of milk, and of water. At other times he finds no difficulty in giving a list of the savours, which are eight: sweet, oily, bitter, harsh. pungent, sour, astringent, saline. This list he proposes to reduce to seven—a number which attracts him, he confesses, as most suitable and natural—by striking out 'saline' as perhaps not sufficiently distinct from 'bitter', and he prefers not to include in his list the vinous taste, since this is a blend of 'sweet', 'astringent', and 'harsh.' Yet though he finds the making of the list an easy task.

But taste is not to be explained by classifying and describing the mere stimulants of taste. The character of the recipient, the sensory, function is also to be heeded. If plants are to produce savours, they must concoct or distil juices that are harmonious with our nature. The tongue, by reason of moisture, perceives savours. He seems to hold that it has the faculty of being affected by strongest contrasts, like that of bitter and sweet, at one and the same time, and these contrary effects, he states, are not to be understood as occurring, the one in one part of the tongue, and the other in another part, but both together in one and the same part. Elsewhere he speaks of the different organic effects which the different savours cause in us, as well as of the like effects which, in different persons, very different stimuli may exceptionally induce. Yet in spite of this difference of origin, he is confident that the experiences which we thus call the same are intrinsically the same in quality. The region of taste, finally, is specifically mentioned as one of those in which there is need that the organ be 'neutral' beforehand in order adequately to perceive: a savour already there blunts the sense.

Doctrine of Touch

Of Theophrastus's doctrine of touch we are almost wholly ignorant, save in so far as it is implied in his general account of perception. We there saw that he perhaps grouped taste and touch together as senses which operate by 'touch'. And holding as he did to the reality of objects independent of our sensory organs, it is not surprising to have him mention specifically heat and cold as probably possessing an objective reality, rather than an existence merely as effects in our senses. Cold and heat by their very nature tend to move, respectively, upward and downward; lightness and heaviness are not, as Plato held, relative and dependent on locality; they have an existence that is absolute. He is also familiar with the other common contrasts between tactual objects —namely, that of hard and soft, and of rough and smooth. His general doctrine that sense perception always involves some intermediary between object and sensory organ does not seem to have been surrendered by Theophrastus, any more than by Aristotle, even in the case of touch; although, as we have just seen, there were certain senses that operated by touch or contact, in the looser meaning of the term. The organic sensations of dizziness, to which reference has already been made when speaking of Theophrastus's account of vision, were considered and an attempt was made at a physiological explanation.

Pleasure and Pain

For Theophrastus pleasure is the normal accompaniment of what is in accord with Nature. As a rule, therefore, we take pleasure in things, since the common course of our functions is inevitably 'natural' and not antagonistic to nature. And any particular function, like perception or understanding, may also be regarded as more intimately conjoined with pleasure than with pain. Yet we must not press our principle too far, and hold that these functions never bring pain; for perception often is accompanied by pain. But with the idea that pain is somehow involved in every operation of our senses, Theophrastus has no patience; such a doctrine is unreasonable, he holds, and is refuted by the plain facts of observation. But excessive stimulation, just because it disturbs the nice correspondence which perception normally presupposes between the sense-organs and their objects, is destructive and therefore causes pain.

Since pleasure is thus the accompaniment and expression of what is in harmony with nature, there is implied, at least distantly, that all those other things that are in accord with nature—such as are better, or in health (to give his own examples)—are also more closely allied with pleasure; and their opposites, with pain. But this mutual adjustment also implies that pleasantness or unpleasantness, like sense perception, is not an absolute property in the object, but is due to the object's relation to the organism, is due to the effect it has upon the organic condition. Especially in the case of food, where the needs of life are so varied as we pass from creature to creature, may we expect an inconstancy or even a reversing of the pleasurable or painful accompaniment. What furthers the life and gives pleasure in one case, hinders life and is repugnant in another. The lower animals in particular are commonly ruled in their attractions and aversions by the meaning of the object as food: few or none of them seek odour for its own sake, but only incidentally because it is the odour of something that is good as food; those objects that promise nourishment to the animals have for them a pleasant odour, and those that in their nature are antagonistic are offensive to their smell.

But with us this is not invariably the case. It is true that many an odour is pleasant to us, as to the animals, because it suggests what we desire as food. But we seek certain odours also for their own sake,—for example, the fragrance of flowers. And now we become aware of the complication of pleasure and of unpleasantness, since fragrant things may be distasteful, and savoury things may have an offensive smell. This partial independence of smell from taste in our case, since odours may be sought for their own sake, reminds us of Theophrastus's similar judgment regarding the perceptive act: its exercise may be sought by us for its own sake, and quite apart from any desire we may have directly for the thing perceived.

Finally, among the varied connections of pleasure and pain, Theophrastus notes that these experiences when excessive produce changes in the humours of the body; and when, under the sway of pleasure and pain, these humours affect the seat of respiration, there may be a complete suspension of consciousness. He also mentions pleasure and pain, along with inspiration as 'principia' of music; for these can turn the voice from its habitual mode and lift it to the plane of beauty. Finally, he rejects Plato's doctrine that some pleasures are false; on the contrary Theophrastus maintains that all are true,'— that is, that they really are pleasures whatever in other respects may be our judgment regarding them.

We have thus in some measure seen how perception and the special senses and pleasure and pain appeared to Theophrastus. And this prepares us to observe more justly the method of exposition and of criticism in his writing On the Senses; we become aware of the atmosphere of knowledge and prejudgment through which this careful student must view the work of others.

He methodically divides his writing into two parts, of which the first is on the sensory and physiological processes, while the second part is on the objects and stimuli, the more physical aspects of sensation. The men to whom his attention is confined are eight in number: Parmenides, Empedocles, Alcmaeon, Anaxagoras, Clidemus, Diogenes of Apollonia, Democritus, and Plato. And these appear to him to possess unequal importance. Of the ninety-one sections into which the text of the fragment has been divided, he gives but one to Clidemus, and but two to Alcmaeon, and two to Parmenides. He presents another group—Diogenes, Anaxagoras, and Plato— to each of whom he gives about equal space, namely ten or eleven sections,—many times the space he assigns either to Parmenides or to Alcmaeon, and yet small in comparison with what still others receive. Empedocles, with eighteen sections, has a very important place; while to Democritus falls the lion's share of attention: the account of his work extends through thirty-four sections, more than a third of the entire work.

Yet in all, the space he uses is extremely small. One cannot but acknowledge Theophrastus's extraordinary skill in giving on so reduced a scale so full and faithful a picture of the doctrines of these men. We admit this skill even while he stirs our impatience by begrudging us an extra word where one would gladly have had, by a phrase, some besetting doubt dispelled. One also would gladly have had from him, now and then, a word of admiration. It would perhaps be too much to expect of him a judgment as noble and almost impassioned as that which even Aristotle cannot repress at the opening of his great Psychology; but there are occasions when he might have half revealed some quiet glow of pleasure in the truth struck out sharp and new in the doctrines he reports. We know, for example, that Theophrastus held that, not things that are alike, but only opposites, affect each other. Yet he gives never a word of greeting to this doctrine at the moment when he unbares it in another. And again we find him urging as of great significance the principle that pleasure is the sign and utterance of what is normal, or 'in accord with nature.' Yet he can report to us such a principle almost beginning its life in Diogenes of Apollonia and more fully grown in Plato, but gives it no mark of recognition. At times, however, we find faint praise, half lost in condemnation, as when, after calling it childish, he says of Diogenes' theory of vision, that it at least in a measure succeeds in refuting certain false proposals, although it does not itself attain the truth.

It is not to Theophrastus's present treatise, then, that one will go for expressed appreciation, but rather for a dispassionate and marvellously impartial report of his man, at the close of which, Theophrastus suddenly changes from reporter into critic. He turns upon the one he has brought before us, raining upon him blows as of tempered steel. And it is difficult to find any personal element here entering. To those who are nearer to his own beliefs, his face is as grim as to the opposition. Thus we know that the dispute regarding perception, whether its operation was by similarity or by contrast, was regarded by him as of great importance; in the case of every one, Theophrastus is looking for his stand upon this question, and at the beginning of his writing he makes this the one great principle of classifying the men whose doctrines he describes. Moreover, his own sympathies, while divided, as we know, were rather with the 'contrast' party. Yet he criticises Anaxagoras with great severity,—with perhaps almost as great severity as appears when he criticises Plato, whom he places with those who favour similarity. Yet with Plato he seems oftener to miss the point, oftener to fight over words, as though there were here some especial want of sympathy. But if twice as much space is given to refuting Empedocles' ideas as to their exposition, we cannot well attribute this to animus. It is clear that Empedocles and Democritus were more interesting to him, perhaps because their doctrines of perception were so picturable, so frankly mechanical, so contrary to his own ways of thought, and they offered such happy marks for his weapons of offence. There can be little doubt that Theophrastus relished his thrusts into the vitals of these men.

We therefore must take Theophrastus here as we find him,—a reviewer with the tribal marks: less sedulous in discovering the merits than in pointing to the defects of the men over whom his cold eye ranges. In much of his other work the interest is more constructive, more single in the aim to let fact and truth speak for themselves, less controversial; but here he lends his support to a custom, —of which he was by no means the father nor the last child,—of approaching in the spirit of a disputant whatever is even distantly connected with philosophy. Of his present work, forty-one of the ninety-one sections are given to criticism; and the case of Empedocles already mentioned, where the criticism is about double the length of the exposition, is almost paralleled by his treatment of Anaxagoras. Yet we may be grateful not only that his eagerness for the fray led him so little to misrepresent his adversary,—but that even in his destructive criticism he showed on the whole so admirable a method, having such definite standards of measuring the work of his great forerunners. Some attempt to observe the principles which guided him in his skilful refutations may perhaps seem here appropriate.

He had, as I have already attempted to set forth, a definite 'point of view' in considering sense perception; we should perhaps rather speak of his 'points of view'.

It must be remembered that if the judgment is right which takes our present to be but a fragment of the work in many books, it is possible that Theophrastus wrote another work in a single book, whose title is given in Diogenes Laertius. If this was a separate work, he doubtless gave expression in it to his constructive ideas upon sense perception, and this would explain his silence upon many a point in the fragment we possess.

For he had more than a single principle or dogma that seemed immovable under his feet,—various convictions upon perception, that need not all again be told. But to some which he used most commonly and with most effect in these criticisms, it will perhaps be pardonable briefly to refer; for we shall soon pass on.

An explanation of sense perception must for him make clear the nature of the object and of the stimulus as external and independent realities. Both Plato and Democritus in their account of the action of the senses fail to satisfy him in this respect. Yet he is equally unsatisfied by a theory that describes merely the object and the stimulus. Explanation is rightly seen to be an intricate affair, and must state the character of the sense-organ and set forth its correspondence with its object. If one would explain how we perceive the external world, he must set forth the mutual relation between sense-organ and sense-object, rather than the character of either of these two terms in isolation. Such is one portion of his plan of criticism. Farther he uses against the theory that perception is due to a kinship or similarity between the object and our senses,—against Empedocles in particular, —the principle that 'like' is not affected by ' like' but only by its opposite —a principle which had perhaps been implied in the thought of Democritus, and which had been acutely discussed by his own great teacher Aristotle.

In attacking Democritus's doctrine that one person's senses attain no more, nor less, truth than another's, he rests his case on the principle that better and worse are not in us alone, but are active in the arrangement of the world; that certain events and conditions are in accord with the nature of things, while others are discordant and this idea he employs also against Anaxagoras's contention that pain is present in every act of perception. What conforms to Nature tends toward what is good; and any explanation which implies that natural powers are aimless or move constantly toward what is harmful must be abandoned. These latter are appeals to principles wider than any special doctrine of perception, as is also his appeal against

Democritus's view that, in hearing, the sound is spread to every nook and cranny of the body. Theophrastus here urges that the causal relation is not the same as that of concomitance: "for if the rest of the body is somehow affected conjointly with the organ of hearing", he says, "it by no means follows that the perception depends upon the body as a whole."

We have, in this, passed quite beyond his own special doctrine of perception, as a standard by which others' theories may be judged. And now, continuing in this wider region, we see prominent his demand that a theory shall internally be simple and consistent. He is troubled by what seems to him inconstancy in several of the earlier psychologists, and for this reason they suffer his condemnation. Democritus would in general explain the effect of a sensory stimulus by the shape of its constituent atoms; but, Theophrastus points out, he is also found explaining the effect by their size, or their position. He ascribes a particular atomic shape to each of the colours save green, and this one colour he explains in quite another way.' He holds that the kinship with the organ of sight is of prime importance for vision, and yet illogically declares that sight depends on colour-contrast, implying that colours of the eyes' own hue are not reflected in them. And so of other Democritean explanations. The inconsistency of Empedocles, too, is shown,—that he holds to a sensuous effluence from bodies; yet this could not always have been in keeping with the operation of his principle of Love. And similarly in Plato's case: if he adopts figure as a means of explaining heat, let him rely on figure, then, to explain cold; if he adopts, to explain vision, the idea that certain particles fit into the sense-organ, or 'correspond' with it, let him use this idea for all the senses.

Not far from this demand for inner harmony, yet passing somewhat beyond, Theophrastus employs a logical 'razor' and requires that a theory display economy; that it use no more principles of explanation than are strictly needed. Thus he condemns Empedocles for introducing the idea of likeness between organ and stimulus to explain perception, when he has already explained it by contrast, And Democritus needlessly introduces the idea of wax like impressions on the air to explain our sight of objects, when he has already supposed that there is an emanation from the object, which could convey the object's form. Furthermore, if our sight of objects is due to an emanation from them, why all this care to explain the difference between white and black by the internal structure of the objects, by minute passages that in one case are straight and in the other case are zig-zag? And to his more formal requirements of sound explanation might be added his demand for accurate classification and definition, —the demand that tilings that are distinct should not be confused in terms —'white', for example, with 'transparent' or 'brilliant'—as well as the obvious requirement that we should be able to understand what an author means.

But a favourite mode of criticism with Theophrastus has regard less to mere form, and more to fact and observation—a mode with which the modern scientist would feel full sympathy. He refutes many of these ancient the-theories by showing that their implications are contrary to fact. Thus—to give but a few examples,—Empedocles' theory of perception, which assumes a close fitting of material particle to particle, would be satisfied by purely physical mixture, and all things that mix should accordingly perceive. And if the presence of many elements in some part of our bodies makes for perception, then bone and hair should be sensitive, for in them too are all the elements. Furthermore, were Anaxagoras correct in his view that sight is fully explained by the reflection in the eye, many a lifeless thing would see; for there is a reflected image in water, in bronze, and in many another thing. The assumption of a due proportion between breath and odours, which Diogenes employed in the explanation of smell, would require that we perceive odour with the breath in our chest, and not solely with that in our nostrils. Nor can the greater purity of the air that is breathed by man account for his intellectual superiority to the brutes; for then mountaineers would surpass plainsmen, and birds would surpass us all.

But in many a case Theophrastus, in order to find a theory absurd, hardly feels it necessary to develop the theory's implications and compare these with the facts; he points out that the theory contradicts the facts are lost in its very statement. The theory of Empedocles, for example, that keenness of smell goes directly with greater inhalation is plainly against the fact that in sickness or at hard labour, the mere amount of breathing is of no avail. Nor is he right in attributing intelligence directly to the blood; for many animals are bloodless, and in others the sense-organs are often the least supplied with blood. Anaxagoras's doctrine that perception is always accompanied by pain, is refuted by the patent fact that perception is often neutral and at times is clearly pleasurable.

Finally in cataloguing the variety of directions from which Theophrastus makes his attack, examples should be given of those criticisms which point out not so much that the theory contradicts the facts, as that it would leave obvious facts quite unexplained. Empedocles' use of likeness and unlikeness, for example, does not account for the clear difference between thought and pleasure and perception, all of which, upon Empedocles' principle, are effects of 'likeness'; and between pain and ignorance, which are due to 'difference.' And against Anaxagoras's theory that vision is due to the reflection in the eye, is the fact that in this reflection we find no adequate representation of size, motion, and distance, nor of the many contrasting objects we see at once.

But now in taking leave of Theophrastus's method, let us for a moment enquire as to the justice of these his skilful assaults.

In general his criticisms, as already has been said, are of a high order; they point out unerringly the failure in many an early essay at explanation, and remove from our minds any lingering sense that the futility, the childishness, of much of this scientific speculation was never felt until the dawn of modern science. Yet we must know that Theophrastus was not always of clearest judgment, and at times would make the better reason in his adversary appear worse, or would tilt for a mere word.

In illustration of these less creditable attempts, one might perhaps include his objection to Plato's definition of soft, as that which yields to our flesh. "But if whatever is yielding is soft", interposes Theophrastus, " evidently water and air and fire are soft. And since he says that any substance is yielding that has a small base, fire would be the softest of all. But none of these statements is widely accepted, nor in general is it held that a thing is soft that moves freely around and behind the entering body; bat only what yields in ' depth' without free change of place." Equally unprofitable in his remark regarding Plato that " it is incorrect to liken odour to vapour and mist, and to say that vapour and mist are identical. Nor does he himself seem actually so to regard them; for vapour is in transition from water to air, he says, while mist is in transition from air to water. And yet in regard to mist the very opposite is generally held to be the fact; for when mist arises water disappears." And unpenetrating, too, is Theophrastus's observation regarding Plato, that in his theory of vision "he agrees in general with Empedocles, since his idea that particles are proportioned to the organ of sight amounts to the thought that certain elements fit into the passages of sense." It is difficult to understand how Theophrastus, basing, as he did, his account of Plato almost wholly on the Timaeus, could have failed to see that the difference here between Plato and Empedocles exceeded by far their likeness. Theophrastus, like Aristotle, furthermore, fails to appreciate Plato's penetrating originality in regard to the conceptions 'heavy' and 'light'. The idea of relativity here, which we should accept as facing in the right direction, is for Theophrastus, who would have things heavy and light per se, merely a blunder.

Yet these misadventures are not confined to his criticism of Plato, though here they are most evident. He more than once fails in judgment regarding Democritus. Thus Theophrastus is rather a formal logician than a penetrating scientist when he criticises as redundant Democritus's use of both emanations and air-prints. For are these not addressed, we might urge, to very different aspects of our vision: the wax-like air-print to explain how we see the form of things; the emanation to explain our perception of its colour? A seal-like impression, we should have to say to Theophrastus, does not convey the hue; neither does a mere effluence, as we know well in the case of odour, convey the shape. And again his words sound as of a mere logician rather than as coming from a sympathetic interpreter of science when he says of Democritus's account of taste, that "the one glaring inconsistency running through the whole account is, that he no sooner declares savours to be subjective effects in sense than he distinguishes them by their figures. . . . For the figure cannot possibly be a subjective effect." It might well be that for Democritus this was a 'glaring inconsistency', but it was a failing that leaned to virtue's side; for tastes are at once sensuous effects in us and are definite external stimuli; and for Democritus to observe and in a measure to do justice to this double existence which they have was better than for him to follow blindly the leading of his theory.

Such were the less happy turns of Theophrastus's critical judgment. But in closing this portion of our work, our minds may better rest upon attempts more fortunate; and these are not difficult to discover.

Of clear excellence is his criticism of Anaxagoras's idea that larger sensory organs imply better sensory power. "When Anaxagoras says that larger animals have better powers of sense, and that sense perception varies in general with the size of the organs of sense, one of these propositions raises the question whether small animals or large animals have better powers of sense. For it would seem to be essential to keener sense perception that minute objects should not escape it. And we might reasonably suppose, too, that an animal with power to discern smaller objects could also discern the larger. Indeed it is held that, so far as certain of the senses are concerned, small animals are superior to large ones; and in so far, consequently, the perceptive power of the larger animals would be inferior. But on the other hand, if it appear that many objects actually do escape the senses of small animals, then the sense perception of larger animals is superior."

Of equal excellence is his attack on Democritus's theory that the form of objects is conveyed to our eyes by seal like impressions on the air. What merciless advance upon the foe, what cold dismemberment, what burial of the remains!

"Now in the first place," begins our critic, "this imprint upon the air is an absurdity. For the substance receiving such an imprint must have a certain consistence and not be 'fragile' even as Democritus himself, in illustrating the character of the impression, says that it is as if one were to take a mould in wax. In the second place, an object could make a better imprint upon water than upon air, since water is denser. While the theory would require us to see more distinctly an object in water, we actually see it less so. But assuming that this absurdity be fact, and the air is moulded like wax that is squeezed and pressed, how does the reflection in the eye come into existence, and what is its character? When several objects are seen in one and the same place, how can so many imprints be made upon the self-same air? And again, how could we possibly see each other? For the imprints would inevitably clash, since each of them would be facing the person from whom it sprung. All of which gives us pause.

"Furthermore, why does not each person see himself? For the imprints from ourselves would be reflected in our own eyes quite as they are in the eyes of our companions, especially if these imprints directly face us and if the effect here is the same as with an echo,—since Democritus says that in the case of the echo the vocal sound is reflected back to him who utters it. Indeed the whole idea of imprints made on the air is extravagant. For we should be forced to believe, from what he says, that all bodies are producing imprints in the air, and that great numbers of them are sending their impressions across one another's path,—a state of things at once embarrassing to sight and improbable on other grounds. If the impression moreover endures, we ought to see bodies that are out of sight and remote,—if not by night, at all events by day. And yet it would be but fair to assume that these imprints would persist at night, since then the air is so much cooler.

"Possibly, however, the reflection in the eye is caused by the sun, in sending light in upon the visual sense in the form of rays—as Democritus seems to mean. For the idea that the sun 'drives the air from itself, and, in thus repelling, condenses it' as he says,—this is indefensible; since the sun by its very nature disperses the air."

Such are a few of his many just objections. And while we have lingered long before letting Theophrastus speak entirely for himself, yet the delay will not have been vain if we should have caught some glimpse of his manner and success of criticism and of his varied knowledge and prepossessions in regard to sense perception. For thus we should have some portion of the background against which he viewed the work of the founders of Greek empirical psychology and of those who added to the labour of these founders, down to the time of Aristotle.

Post-Aristotelian Philosophy: The Stoics by Alexander Grant

DOWN to the time of Aristotle, Greek philosophy may be said to have lived apart. It contained within itself a gradual progress and culmination of thought, but the great philosophers who were the authors of this progress moved on a level far above the ordinary modes of comprehension. After the death of Aristotle a new spectacle is presented— philosophy no longer an exclusive and esoteric property of the schools, but spreading its results over the world.

The immediate cause which brought about this change— which turned philosophy into a universal leaven, leavening, under one form or another, the thoughts of all cultivated men—must be sought for in the changed position of Ethics in relation to the other parts of philosophy. In spite of the exclusive attention of Socrates to ethical investigations, in spite of the exclusive effort of the Cynics and Cyrenaics to promulgate respectively a conception of practical life for the individual, in spite of the moral earnestness of Plato and the brilliant contributions to anthropology, in the way of accumulation, analysis, and classification of data, made by Aristotle—Ethics had hitherto continued to occupy a really subordinate position in the mind of Greece. With Socrates the paramount interest had been the attainment of universal conceptions; with him Ethics were rather the field for scientific experiments in method, than an ultimate end to. which all else was to be subordinated.

The one-sided Socraticists had been regarded as merely exceptional and paradoxical nonconformists to the ordinary mode of life. In the mind of Plato Ethics blended themselves with aspirations after a perfectly ordered State, and to him the contemplation of all time and all existence under the light of idealism was as dear as was the education of the individual soul. Aristotle, in the process of reconstructing all the departments of thought and knowledge, took Ethics, so to speak, in his stride. He allotted to man, as a practical being, an important position in the scale of the universe, but still he said that the good attainable in a life of moral virtue was secondary to that attainable in a life of philosophy (Eth, x. viii. i); that 'the end-in-itself' for a State was more beautiful and divine than that for an individual (i. ii. 8); and (as Eudemus expressed it, Eth. vi. vii. 4), that there are in the universe many things diviner than man.' Such sayings imply that Ethics are inferior in practical interest to Politics, and in intellectual interest to the speculative branches of philosophy. But after Aristotle, the order which he had given to the hierarchy of the sciences became subverted. All considerations of the State now dropped out of sight, as of a subject no longer capable of being entertained; Ethics came to the fore-front, as if the practical interests of the individual were of paramount and absorbing importance; and all other departments of inquiry, whether logical, metaphysical, or physical, were cultivated only as subsidiary to the one great object of obtaining a theory for the regulation of individual life.

These features were equally characteristic of the two great post-Aristotelian schools, the Stoic and the Epicurean.

To account for them it does not seem quite sufficient to refer, with Zeller, to the political condition of Greece. The loss of independence in the Greek States might reasonably account for the abandonment of Politics as a science; but the times do not seem to have been dangerous and oppressive, such as would force the mind by fears and interruptions away from philosophical inquiry. Political freedom does not appear to be an absolute necessity for freedom of speculation, for in Germany the greatest achievements in philosophy were made at a time when the liberties of the people were most scanty. And in Athens during the third century B.C., there was a vast amount of active philosophizing on almost all the great subjects, though these now received a peculiar turn in their mode of treatment. And Plutarch speaks of the early Stoics, Zeno, Cleanthes, and Chrysippus, as living at Athens as though they had eaten of the lotus, spell-bound on a foreign soil, enamoured of leisure, and spending their long lives in books, and walks, and discourses. Athens was still a genial home for philosophy 'native to famous wits, or hospitable, in her sweet recess, and other causes,' besides political circumstances, must be sought for the peculiar character of the philosophical schools that now arose within her walls. That they exhibited a decline in force of thought, is indubitable: but in this world it appears as if a succession of great geniuses can never be long maintained. In Germany the great idealistic systems of philosophy were succeeded by a strong reaction in the direction of materialism. And in Greece the same phenomenon presented itself after the death of Aristotle. Zeno and Epicurus displayed an equal aversion to that idealism which characterizes the thought of Aristotle no less than Plato; each denied the existence of anything immaterial; and each reverted to the physical system of a pre-Socratic philosopher as a more reasonable explanation of the world than that which Plato or Aristotle had given.

Zeno thus espoused the physics of Heraclitus, and Epicurus those of Democritus. Besides this reaction towards pre-Socratic materialism, there was another reaction in which both these philosophers shared, namely, towards the pre-Aristotelian individualism of the Cynics and Cyrenaics. The character of the times certainly favoured the rehabilitation and development of this principle; the scope for public life and action was gone, and thus individuality supplanted the idea of citizenship. To find out the way of happiness for the individual soul, became now, not one problem among many, but the one great problem for philosophy, to which all others were to be secondary and subordinate. Thus a new era of thought commenced with Zeno and Epicurus, in which Ethics was elevated to the first place and became the architectonic science. And the causes for this, so far as we have reviewed them, were common to both Zeno and Epicurus, consisting in a decline of personal ability and philosophic power, in an inability to keep up to the level of the speculative and idealistic systems, and also in the circumstances of the times, which encouraged a monkish exclusiveness of attention to the subjective and practical well-being of the individual soul.

But there was another special cause which contributed greatly to give its peculiar character to the Stoical school, and which is the source of much of the interest that attaches to the history of that school. In a former edition of this Essay it was suggested that the striking features and attitude exhibited by the Stoical doctrine were attributable to the Race from which its founders sprang. This idea has subsequently been accepted and worked out,' and may be now considered to have been established. If we cast oar eyes on a list of the early Stoics and their native places, we cannot avoid noticing how universally the leaders of this school came from the East to Athens, how many of them came from Semitic towns or colonies. Zeno was from Citium, a Phoenician colony in Cyprus, and himself belonged to the Semitic race, as is testified by the sobriquet of 'the Phoenician' commonly applied to him. Of his disciples, Persaeus came also from Citium; Herillus was from Carthage; Athenodorus from Tarsus; Cleanthes. The chief disciples of Cleanthes were Antigonus, and Chrysippus from Soli in Cilicia. Chrysippus was succeeded by Zeno of Sidon, and Diogenes of Babylon; the latter taught Antipater of Tarsus, who taught Panaetius of Rhodes, who taught Posidonius of Apamea in Syria. There was another Athenodorus, from Cana in Cilicia; and the early Stoic Archedemus is mentioned by Cicero as belonging to Tarsus. The names of Nestor, Athenodorus, Cordylion, and Heraclides, may be added to the list of Stoical teachers furnished by Tarsus. Seleucia sent forth Diogenes; Epiphania Euphrates; Scythopolis Basilides; Ascalon Antibius; Tyre Antipater; Sidon; Ptolemais Diogenes. We see then what an Oriental aspect this catalogue presents. Not a single Stoic of note was a native of Greece proper. From Tyre and Sidon, and Ptolemais and Ascalon and Apamea, from Babylon and Carthage, the future 'doctors of the

Stoic fur' come flocking to Athens. No country more Greek than Rhodes or Phrygia, is the home of any. On the whole, Cilicia and the Semitic colony in Cyprus are the chief headquarters whence the leaders of this sect were derived.

These facts give us an insight into the fundamental and essential character of Stoicism. Its essence consists in the introduction of the Semitic temperament and a Semitic spirit into Greek philosophy.

The meeting of Eastern and Western ideas had been prepared by the conquests of Alexander, and the production of Stoicism was one of its first fruits. We moderns have all been imbued with the Semitic spirit in its highest manifestations by the pages of Holy Writ. Other manifestations of that spirit, as for instance the Mahomedan religion, exhibit it as an intense, but narrow, earnestness, averse on the whole to science and art, but tending to enthusiasm and even fanaticism for abstract ideas of religion or morality. The Semitic spirit found a new and favourable field for its development in Athens at the close of the fourth century B.C. If philosophy in general was then tending from other causes to the exaltation of Ethics over Metaphysics, this tendency just suited the Semitic moral earnestness. Ethics were taken up by the Phoenician Zeno, and came out from his hands with a new aspect. A phase of thought now appears for the first time on Hellenic soil, in which the moral consciousness of the individual—the moral ego —is made the centre and starting-point. Such a point of view, with various concomitant ideas, such as duty and responsibility, and self-examination, and the sense of shortcoming, and moral self-cultivation, is familiar to us in the Psalms of David and afterwards in the writings of St. Paul, but it was not to be found in the conversations of Socrates, nor in the dialogues of Plato, nor in the Ethics of Aristotle.

It was alien indeed from the childlike and unconscious spirit of the Hellenic mind, with its tendency to objective thought and the enjoyment of nature. Our own views in modern times have been so much tinged with Hebraism, that the highest degree of moral consciousness seems only natural to us, and thus Stoicism, which introduced this state of feeling to the ancient Hellenic world, may be said to have formed a transition step between Greek philosophy and the modern ethical point of view. So it is that in many modern books of morals, and even in many practical sermons, we come upon much that has a close affinity with the modes of thinking of the ancient Stoics, while with the modes of thinking of Plato and Aristotle such productions have rarely any affinity at all. And this is the secret of the interest that Stoicism has for modern times.

Epicurus, the son of Athenian parents, handled the problem of his epoch—that of the well-being of the individual soul—in a sense widely different from that of Zeno. Much as the two schools, Stoicism and Epicurism, had originally in common, they each followed out their fundamental tendencies so as to diverge ultimately into the strongest contrast and to stand in the sharpest antithesis to each other. If we ask on what does this antithesis rest? we shall find that it rests on the twofold essence of man, as a thinking and as a feeling subject; as consisting, on the one hand, of spirit, or free and self-determined thought; and, on the other hand, of nature, or an existence determined by physical laws expressing themselves in the sensuous feelings and desires. These two sides of man's being may often stand in opposition to each other; or again, they may be harmonized so as to give either the one side or the other the precedence and authority. Either we may say a thing is good because it is pleasant and thus refer the decision to the natural feelings; or we may say 'it is pleasant because it is good,' and thus refer the decision to the inner spirit or reason. How far these two sentences actually express the leading principles of the Stoic and the Epicurean schools, we may best see by considering the ideal of man which they each proposed to themselves. The Epicurean ideal was a being moving harmoniously according to natural impulses; one, in short, in whom the spirit and thought should rather form a part of the natural life than prominently control it. The Stoic ideal, on the contrary, was a being in whom the natural impulses and desires should be absolutely subjected to the laws of abstract thought. Epicurism is essentially Greek and essentially Pagan; the beautiful and genial Greek mythology is but a deification of the natural powers and impulses. Stoicism is a reaction against this; it consists in an inner life, in a drawing away from the body, and in disregarding as worthless and of no moment the 'law in the members.' Epicurism and Stoicism both received as an inheritance the results of Grecian speculation, but in both, the moral attitude was what was essential. Of both it has been truly said that they were less and more than philosophy. Less, because they were thoroughly unspeculative in their character, and indeed consisted in the popularizing of speculation; more, because they were not mere systems of knowledge, but a principle for the whole of life. They soon lost their local and restricted character as schools; they assimilated to themselves more and more broadly human thought, and became 'the two great confessions of faith of the historical world.'

Thus were these two ideas set against each other. Regarding, however, Stoicism, with its weakness and its strength, as far the more interesting and important, as it is, of course, also far the higher tendency of the two, we shall henceforth, in tracing its history, only incidentally allude to the fortunes of its rival.

In the history of Stoicism, the following parts of the subject seem naturally to stand apart from each other, and to demand in some sort a separate treatment: First, the period of the formation of the Stoical dogma in Athens, from Zeno to Chrysippus; second, the period of the promulgation of Stoicism and its introduction to the knowledge of other civilized nations; third. Stoicism in the Roman world, its different phases, and its influence on individual thought and on public manners and institutions. The first period of Stoicism takes us down to the year 207 B.C., which was the date of the death of Chrysippus. The chronology of the commencement of this period is difficult to fix. Zeno probably lived till after the year 260 B.C., and he may have been born rather before 340 B.C. It is uncertain whether he came to Athens in his twenty-second or his thirtieth year. On the whole, we may assume that he did not arrive there till after the death of Aristotle, which took place in the year 322 B.C. Chrysippus may possibly in early youth have heard some of the discourses of Zeno; but Cleanthes, who succeeded Zeno as leader of the Porch, was the true link between them. By these three the Stoical doctrine, properly so called, received its completion. Nothing was afterwards added to it, except the eclectic amalgamation of other doctrines. These three personages come before us with great distinctness. The anecdotes that have been handed down about them, though perhaps in some cases mythical, are at all events highly symbolic, and give us a very definite conception of their separate characteristics.

Zeno is described as a slight, withered little fellow, of a swarthy complexion, and with his neck on one side. The story goes, that in trading to Athens he was shipwrecked at the Piraeus, and was thus 'cast on to the shores of philosophy.' Going up to the city, he sat down at the stall of a bookseller, where he read the second book of the Memorabilia of Xenophon, and asked with enthusiasm where such men lived.' Crates, the Cynic, happened to be passing at the moment, and the bookseller cried, 'Follow him.' Zeno then studied under Crates, but held himself aloof from the extravagant unseemliness of Cynicism. He is also said to have studied under the Megarians, Stilpo, Cronus, and Philo, and under the Academicians, Xenocrates and Polemo. After twenty years, he opened his school in the Stoa Poecile, the porch adorned with the frescoes of Polygnotus. Zeno appears to have impressed the Athenians with the highest admiration for his character. Their treatment of him was a contrast to their treatment of Socrates. It is perhaps an apocryphal tradition which relates that they deposited the keys of their citadel with him, as being the most trustworthy person; but it may be true that they decreed to him a golden crown, a brazen statue, and a public entombment. In extreme old age he committed suicide. Cleanthes, the disciple of Zeno, was perhaps the most zealous disciple that a philosopher ever had. He is said to have been originally a boxer, and to have come to Athens with four drachmas in his possession.

By his strength, his endurance, and his laborious life, he acquired the name of 'the New Hercules.' 'Falling in with Zeno,' it is said, 'he took the philosophy most bravely.' He wrote notes of his master's lectures on potsherds and the blade bones of oxen, not being able to afford to purchase tabtablets. He was summoned before the Areopagus to give an account of his way of living, since his whole days were passed in philosophy, and he had no ostensible calling nor means of support. He proved to his judges that he drew water by night for a gardener, and ground the corn for a flour-dealer, and thus earned a maintenance. The story goes on that his judges, on hearing this account, voted him ten minae, which the rigid Zeno forbade him to accept. There is something quaint about the whole personality of Cleanthes. He was nicknamed 'the Ass,' for his stubborn patience. He seems to have left the impression that it was this indomitable perseverance, rather than the superiority of his genius, that gave him precedence over other noteworthy disciples of Zeno. ' High thinking,' however, appears to have accompanied the 'plain living' of Cleanthes. His reflections on Destiny, and his Hymn to Jupiter, will best be treated of hereafter. When asked, 'What is the best way to be rich?' he answered, 'To be poor in desires.' No reproaches or ridicule ever ruffled the sweetness and dignity of his presence. His calm bearing, when satirized on the stage by the comic poet Sositheus, caused the spectators to applaud him and to hiss off Sositheus. The idea of death seems to have been long present to his mind. Being taunted with his old age, he said, 'Yes, I am willing to be gone, but when I see myself scund in every part, writing and reading, I am again tempted to linger.' The story of his death is characteristic. Having suffered from an ulcer on the tongue, he was advised by his physician to abstain from eating for a while in order to facilitate the cure. Having fasted for two days he was completely cured, and his physician bade him return to his usual course of life, but he said that 'Since he had got so far on the road, it would be a pity not to finish the journey;' so continuing his abstinence, he died.

Hardly any personal details of the life of Chrysippus have come to us. On the other hand, we have more fragments of his actual writings than of those of all the early Stoics put together. In Chrysippus the man seems swallowed up in the writer and disputer. He is said to have been slight in person, so that his statue in the Cerameicus was totally eclipsed by a neighbouring equestrian figure, and from this circumstance Carneades nicknamed him Chrysippus. His literary activity was most unrivalled: he wrote above seven hundred and five works on different subjects. Epicurus alone, of the ancient philosophers, outstripped him in voluminousness of writing. He is said to have been keen and able on every sort of subject. He told Cleanthes that he 'only wanted the doctrines and he would soon find out the proofs.' This boast appears to betray a want of earnestness as to the truth, and somewhat too much of the spirit of a dialectician. In this respect Chrysippus must have differed widely from his two distinguished predecessors, with whom Stoicism was above all things a reality and a mode of life. However, there is no doubt that Chrysippus did great service to the Stoic school by embodying their doctrines and stating them in manifold different ways. Hence the saying, "But for Chrysippus, the Porch would never have been." He developed Stoicism on its negative and antagonistic side by arguing with trenchant dialectic against Epicurus and the Academy. We shall see that he really mooted and boldly strove to reconcile some of the deepest and most difficult contradictions of human thought—difficulties which are ever present in modem metaphysics, but which had never truly occupied the ancients before the death of Aristotle.

We know most about Chrysippus from Plutarch's book On the Inconsistencies of the Stoics. It consists really of the inconsistencies of Chrysippus, extracted from various parts of his voluminous writings. This interesting book gives the impression that Plutarch is unphilosophical, though we are not able to exonerate Chrysippus from inconsistency. Such rapid and extensive writing, such a warm spirit of advocacy, such an attempt to round off and complete a doctrine in spite of all difficulties, such a various controversialism, such an elevated theory, paradoxical even in the grandeur of its aims, combined, on the other hand, with an extremely practical point of view—could not fail to give rise to manifold inconsistencies. Chrysippus was inconsistent, just as Seneca afterwards was inconsistent, because it suited the genius of Stoicism to abandon the stern simplicity and unity of a scientific principle. Stoicism became learned, complex, and eclectic; embracing in its grasp a far greater variety of problems than the philosophy of Plato or Aristotle had done, it treated these more loosely, and often oscillated between mere empiricism and a more philosophical point of view.

Taking now the Stoical doctrine as it gradually formed itself during the entire course of the third century B.C., we may proceed to trace its essential features, though in the lack of direct writings of the successive masters of the school we must give up attempting to fix their several contributions, and their differences from each other. Early Stoicism consisted of two elements—the one might be called dynamical: it was the peculiar spirit, tendency, and mental attitude assumed; the other element was material, being an adaptation of the results of existing philosophy. The material side of Stoicism was comparatively unimportant. This it was, however, which caused Cicero to make the mistaken observation that Zeno was no real innovator, but only a reproducer of the Peripatetic doctrines. And indeed it is sufficiently striking at first sight of the Stoical compendia, that their ethic seems a patchwork of Peripatetic and Platonic formulae: their logic, a development of the doctrine of the syllogism; and their physic, a blending of Heraclitus with Aristotle. Yet, in spite of all this, Zeno was no mere eclectic; all that was Peripatetic in his system was the outward, and not the inner and essential part. And in short, the vestiges of previous Greek philosophy existing in Stoical books may be said, mutatis mutandis, to bear the same relation to Stoicism as the vestiges of Jewish and of Alexandrian ideas existing in the New Testament bear to Christianity. What we have called the dynamical element of Stoicism constitutes its real essence. This is derived partly from the idiosyncrasy and perhaps the national characteristics of its founder, partly from the peculiarities of the Cynical school in which it was nurtured.

Zeno agreed with Crates, and Stoicism coincides with the Cynic view thus far, that it makes the starting-point of all thought to be the conception of a life. The setting of this moral and practical conception above all speculative philosophy separates Zeno from the previous schools of Greece. We have now to ask, What is it that distinguishes him from Crates?—what is the essential difference between the Stoic and the Cynic creeds? This is generally stated as if the former were merely a softened edition of the latter. The Cynic said, There is nothing good but virtue; all else is absolutely indifferent. The Stoic said, Yes, but among indifferent things some are preferable to others; health, though not an absolute good, is, on the whole, preferable to sickness; and this, though not an evil, is, on the whole, to be avoided.' Again, it is said that Cynicism is unseemly and brutal, and tramples upon society; Stoicism is more gentle, and outwardly conforms with the world. But this comparison does not go sufficiently deep, and does not explain the facts of the case, for the Stoics were often as paradoxical as the Cynics in denying that anything was a good besides virtue; and if they were outwardly less ferocious, we want to know what was the inward law of their doctrine that made them so. Perhaps we nearest touch the spring of indifference, by observing that Cynicism is essentially mere negation, mere protest against the external world; while Stoicism is essentially positive, essentially constructive, and tends in many ways to leaven the external world. Cynicism despised the sciences, disdained politics, exploded the social institutions, and ridiculed patriotism or the distinctions of country. Zeno, on the contrary, rearranged the sciences according to his views: he enjoined the wise to mix in affairs; and he conceived not a mere negation of patriotic prejudices, but the positive idea of cosmopolitanism. Cynicism, therefore, is a withdrawal from the world into blank isolation, while Stoicism is the withdrawal into an inner life, which forms to its votaries an object of the highest enthusiasm. Hence the elation, often hyperbolical, which tinges the Stoical austerity;

hence the attractiveness of the doctrine and its spread over the world. And connected, too, with the positive and constructive impulse of Stoicism, we may reckon its plastic character, its external eclecticism, and its tendency to be influenced and modified by the course of 'surrounding civilisation. '

Lists have been preserved for us by the ancients of the different formulae in which the Stoical masters expressed the leading principle of life. They are all modifications of- the same idea, that the end for man is to live according to nature.' Nature here means that which is universal—the entire course of the world, as opposed to individual and special ideas and impulses. Until we remember this interpretation, the Stoical formula appears surprising; for how could they enjoin life according to nature, whose whole endeavour was to be superior to nature—to overcome and subdue desire, sorrow, pain, the fear of death, and all that in another sense we are accustomed to call the natural instincts? If nature were taken to mean the involuntary and immediate impulses, then the phrase 'follow nature' would express not the Stoical, but the Epicurean, principle. The Stoical nature was the conception of an abstract and universal order, and was to be apprehended by the discursive Reason. This clear-sightedness and authority of the Reason is, of course, only slowly arrived at, and the Stoics explained their theory by saying that all our duties come from nature, and wisdom among the number. But as, when a man is introduced to anyone, he often thinks more of the person to whom he is introduced than of him who gave the introduction—so we need not wonder that, while it was the instinctive impulses of nature that led us to Wisdom, we hold Wisdom more dear than those impulses by which we arrived at her.' In order to avoid seeming to approximate to the Epicureans, they denied that pleasure and pain are among the principles of nature. In short, starting from nature, the Stoics came round utterly to supplant Nature (in the usual sense), and to substitute in her room pure thought and abstract ideas.

The phrase follow nature, to express the highest kind of life, has never yet established itself in language. One touch of nature makes the whole world kin'—that is, any perfectly simple and instinctive feeling, the very opposite of anything abstract or cultivated. Again, the natural man, as opposed to the spiritual man, denotes something utterly different from the Stoical idea of perfection. Thus, common parlance retains its own associations connected with the term nature, and rejects those of the Stoics. But it is interesting to observe that Bishop Butler has espoused their formula, and has argued that nature does not mean single impulses or desires, but the idea of the constitution of the whole, reason and conscience as regulative principles being taken into consideration. Butler s object in maintaining this position was obviously one relative to his own times. As in appealing to a selfish age he thought it necessary to assert that virtue was not inconsistent with the truest self-love, so also he argued that virtue was not against nature, but in reality man's natural state. He here takes up, just like the Stoics, an abstract ideal of nature; for he makes the basis of his reasoning a proviso that the moral rules of conscience not only exist, but that they have authority—that is, that they control, as they ought to do, the rest of the human principles.

The commonest ideal of virtue according to nature is the picture of mankind in a state of innocence, whether the scene be laid in some far-off island, or remote in point of time, in the golden age of the world. To imagine a primitive and pastoral existence, in which every impulse is virtuous and every impulse is to be obeyed—this is an easy reaction from a vitiated and over-refined civilisation. Some have supposed that the Stoics made this ideal of uncorrupted nature part of their views; but in reality it would not suit the genius of Stoicism to do so. Though they railed at the actual state of the world, their remedy was placed rather in the power of the will, in the effort to progress, than in dreams of a bygone state of innocence. The only allusion which we can trace in their fragments to this conception is a saying of the later Stoic, Posidonius, that in the golden age the government was in the hands of the philosophers.'

The context, however, of this remark, makes it appear rather as a rhetorical praise of philosophy than as a serious piece of doctrine. Seneca, in one of whose epistles it is quoted, comments upon it in an interesting manner. After echoing for a while the strain of Virgil, and praising those times of innocence before the reign of Jupiter, when men slept free and undisturbed under the canopy of heaven, he returns to the true Stoical point of view, and asserts that in those primitive times there was, in fact, no wisdom. If men did wise things, they did them unconsciously. They had not even virtue; neither justice, nor prudence, nor temperance, nor fortitude. It is a profound truth that Seneca perceives—namely, that the mind and the will evoked into consciousness and perfected even by suffering, are greater possessions than the blessings, if they were attainable, of a so-called golden age and state of nature.

Thee Stoical principle of 'life according to nature' would have been a blank formula, were it not for the further exposition of their doctrine which they have left us in their ideal of the Wise Man. This ideal exhibits not the pursuit of wisdom for its own sake—not the excellence of philosophy in and for itself, as Plato and Aristotle used to conceive it, but rather the results of wisdom in the will and character— results which Zeno summed up in the terms an 'even flow of life.' The notion that equanimity is the most essential characteristic of a philosopher is perhaps traceable to this conception of the Stoics; according to whom the Wise Man is infallible, impassive, and invulnerable. And while possessing this external immunity from harm, he is in himself full of divine inspirations—he is alone free, alone king and priest, alone capable of friendship or affection. These and other splendid and exclusive attributes did the Stoics attach to their imaginary sage, till Chrysip-Chrysippus, becoming conscious in one place of the paradoxical character of the picture, allows that he may seem, through the pre-eminent greatness and beauty of his descriptions, to be giving utterance to mere fictions, things transcending man and human nature.'

At the Stoical paradox Horace laughed. Plutarch wrote a book (now lost, but of which the outlines remain) to prove that it surpassed the widest imaginations of the poets. But in truth the curtain was the picture;' the paradox was an essential part of the doctrine. For of necessity these pictures of the inner life are paradoxical. They speak of a boundless freedom and elevation, with which the narrow limits of external reality come into harsh contrast. And in the vaunts of the Stoics we only see what is analogous to one side of Lord Bacon's famous character of a believing Christian, drawn out in paradoxes and seeming contradictions.' He is rich in poverty, and poor in the midst of riches; he believes himself to be a king, how mean soever he be; and how great soever he be, yet he thinks himself not too good to be servant to the poorest saint.'

Some of the qualities of the Stoic ideal seem inferior to the conception of goodness afterwards developed by the school. The Wise Man of Zeno was represented as stern and pitiless, and as never conceding pardon to any one. This forms a great contrast with the gentle and forgiving spirit of Epictetus and Marcus Aurelius. Such harsher traits of the picture are Semitic in tone; they were afterwards discarded during subsequent transmutations of the Stoical principle. More inward meaning is there in the saying, paradoxical as it might appear, that nothing the Wise Man can do would be a crime. Cannibalism, and incest, and the most shocking things, are said to be indifferent to the sage. This, however, though stated so repulsively, can only have meant something resembling the principle that whatever is of faith is no sin.' One of the interests of the Stoical ideal consists in the parallel it affords at many points to different phases of religious feeling. Such for instance is the tendency, more or less vaguely connecting itself with the Stoic doctrine, to divide all the world into the good and the bad, or, as they expressed it, into the wise and the fools—an idea evidently belonging to the inner life, and hard to bring into conformity with external facts. Entirely in the same direction, the Stoics said that short of virtue—in other words short of the standard of perfection—all faults and vices were equal. Chrysippus, indeed, tried to soften down this assertion; but in its extreme form it only reminds us of certain sayings which have been heard in modem times, about the 'worthlessness of morality.' In the presence of a dazzling idea of spiritual perfection, the minor distinctions of right and wrong seem to lose their meaning.

The Stoics, after portraying their Wise Man, were free to confess that such a character did not exist, and indeed never had existed. With small logical consistency, but with much human truth, while they allowed their assertions about the worthlessness of all except absolute wisdom to remain, and always held up this unattained and unattainable ideal, they admitted another conception to stand, though unacknowledged, beside it—namely, the conception of 'advance.' Zeno and the rest, though they do not claim to be wise, yet claimed to be 'advancing.' This notion of conscious moral progress and self-discipline is too familiar now for us easily to believe that it was first introduced into Greece in the third century B.C. It may be said, indeed, to be contained implicitly in Aristotle's theory of habits; but it is in reality the expression of a new and totally different spirit. By this spirit we shall find the later Stoics deeply penetrated. It constituted perhaps the most purely 'moral' notion of antiquity, as implying the deepest associations which are attached to the word moral.

Another great idea, of which the introduction is generally attributed to the Stoics, is the idea of duty; but on consideration, we shall perceive that this, entirely conformable as it was with their point of view, was not all at once enunciated by them, but was only gradually developed in or by means of their philosophy. There were two correlative terms introduced by the early Stoics, signifying the 'suitable' and the 'right.' The 'right' could only be said of actions having perfect moral worth. The 'suitable' included all that fitted in harmoniously with the course of life—everything that could on good grounds be recommended or defended. So much casuistical discussion took place upon what was, or was not, suitable, that a train of associations became attached to the word, associations which were inherited by the Romans. Thus the idea of duty grew up, more belonging, perhaps, to the Roman than to the Greek elements in the Stoic spirit, fostered by a national sternness and a love of law, and ultimately borrowing its modes of expression from the formulae of Roman jurisprudence.

The most prominent conception in the Stoical system being the effort to attain a perfect life in conformity with universal laws, we may now ask what forms the background to this picture. Aristotle and Plato would certainly have conceived to themselves a limited state, essentially Greek in character, the institutions of which should furnish sufficiently favourable conditions for the life of the Wise Man.

Zeno now imagined, what surpassed the Republic of Plato, a universal state, with one government and manner of life for all mankind. This admired polity, which Plutarch calls 'a dream of philosophic statesmanship,' and which, he rhetorically says, was realized by Alexander the Great, owed, no doubt, its origin to the influence upon men's minds produced by the conquests of Alexander. This influence, partly depressing—in so far as it dimin-diminished the sense of freedom, and robbed men of their healthy, keen, and personal interest in politics—was also partly stimulating, since it unfolded a wider horizon, and the possibility of conceiving a universal state. Thus were the national and exclusive ideas of Greece, as afterwards of Rome, changed into cosmopolitanism. The first lesson of cosmopolitanism, that said, 'there is no difference between Greece and barbarians—the world is our city,' must have seemed a mighty revelation. To say this was quite natural to Stoicism, which drawing the mind away from surrounding objects, bids it soar into the abstract and the universal. By denying the reality and the interest of national politics, the moral importance of the individual was immensely enhanced. Ethics were freed from all connection with external institutions, and were joined in a new and close alliance to physics and theology.

    The cosmopolitanism of the Stoics was a cosmopolitanism in the widest etymological sense, for they regarded not the inhabited earth alone but the whole universe, as man's city. Undistracted by political ideas, they placed the individual in direct relation to the laws of the Cosmos. Hence Chrysippus said, that no ethical subject could be rightly approached except from the preconsideration of entire nature and the ordering of the whole.' Hence his regular preamble to every discussion of good, evil, ends, justice, marriage, education, and the like, was some exordium about Pate or Providence. So close and absolute a dependence of the individual upon the Divine First Cause was asserted by the Stoics, that their theological system reminds us, to some extent, of modern Calvinism, or of the doctrines of Spinoza. Body, they said, is the only substance. Nothing incorporeal could act upon what is corporeal, or vice versa. The First Cause of all is God, or Zeus—the universal reason, the world-spirit, which may also be represented as the primeval fire, just as the soul of man, which is an emanation from it, consists of a warm ether. God, by transformation of his own essence, makes the world. All things come forth from the bosom of God, and into it all things will again return, when by universal conflagration the world sinks into the divine fire, and God is again left alone. The universe is a living and rational whole; for how else could the human soul, which is but a part of that whole, be rational and conscious ? If the Cosmos be compared to an individual man, then Providence is like the spirit of a man. Thus all things are very good, being ordered and preordained by the divine reason. This reason is also destiny, which is defined to be 'the law according to which what has been, has been; what is, is; and what shall be, shall be.' The round world hangs balanced in an infinite vacuum. It is made up of four elements—fire and air, which are active powers; water and earth, which are passive materials. Within it are four classes of natural objects—inorganic substances, plants, animals, and rational beings. First and highest among rational beings are the sun and the stars and all the heavenly bodies, which, as Plato and Aristotle used to say, are conscious, reasonable, and blessed existences. These, indeed, are created gods, divine but not eternal. They will at last, like all things else, return into the unity of the primeval fire. Other gods, or rather other manifestations of the one divine principle, exist in the elements and the powers of nature, which, accordingly, are rightly worshipped by the people, and have received names expressive of their different attributes. Heroes, also, with divine qualities, are justly deified; and the Wise Man is divine, since he bears a god within himself. In this city of Zeus, where all is holy, and earth and sky are full of gods, the individual man is but a part of the whole—only one expression of the universal law.

Abstractedly, the theology of the Stoics appears as a materialistic pantheism; God is represented as a fire, and the world as a mode of God. But, practically, this aspect of the creed is softened by two feelings—by their strong sense, first, of the personality of God; and secondly, of the individuality of man. These feelings express themselves in the hymn of Cleanthes, the most devotional fragment of Grecian antiquity. In this hymn, Zeus is addressed as highest of the gods, having many names, always omnipotent, leader of nature, and governing all things by law.

'Thee,' continues the poet, 'it is lawful for all mortals to address. For we are thy offspring, and alone of living creatures possess a voice which is the image of reason. Therefore, I will for ever sing thee and celebrate thy power. All this universe rolling round the earth obeys thee, and follows willingly at thy command. Such a minister hast thou in thy invincible hands, the two-edged, flaming, vivid, thunderbolt. O King, most high, nothing is done without thee either in heaven or on earth, or in the sea, except what the wicked do in their foolishness. Thou makest order out of disorder, and what is worthless becomes precious in thy sight; for thou hast fitted together good and evil into one, and hast established one law that exists for ever. But the wicked fly from thy law, unhappy ones, and though they desire to possess what is good, yet they see not, neither do they hear, the universal law of God. If they would follow it with understanding, they might have a good life. But they go astray, each after his own devices—some vainly striving after reputation, others turning aside after gain excessively, others after riotous living and wantonness. Nay, but, O Zeus, giver of all things, who dwellest in dark clouds, and rulest over the thunder, deliver men from their foolishness. Scatter it from their souls, and grant them to obtain wisdom, for by wisdom thou dost rightly govern all things; that being honoured we may repay thee with honour, singing thy works without ceasing, as is right for us to do. For there is no greater thing than this, either for mortal men or for the gods, to sing rightly the universal law.'

In this interesting fragment we see, above all, a belief in the unity of God. This, Plato and Aristotle had most certainly arrived at. Even in the popular ideas it probably lay behind all polytheistic forms, as being a truth necessary to the mind. But Monotheism here, as in the early Hebrew Scriptures, is co-existent with a mention of other gods besides the one highest God. These are represented as inferior to Zeus, and singing his praises. The human soul is here depicted as deriving all happiness from wisdom and a knowledge of God. The knowledge of God and a devotional regard to Him are mentioned as needs of the human soul, though the knowledge spoken of appears partly under the aspect of an intuition into the universal and impersonal law. When Cleanthes speaks of 'repaying God with honour,' we see a strong assertion of the worth of the individual. Heraclitus had said of old that 'Zeus looks on the wisest man as we look on an ape.' But now the feeling about these things was changed, and Chrysippus even went so far as to say, that the sage is not less useful to Zeus than Zeus is to the sage '—a saying which is rendered less offensive by taking it partly in a metaphysical sense, to mean that the individual is as necessary to the universal law as vice versa.

As strong an assertion as this would seem almost required to counterbalance the absorbing necessarian element in early Stoicism. At first it excites surprise that a system putting so great store on the moral will should on the other hand appear to annihilate it. If all proceeds by destiny, what scope is left for individual action, for self-discipline and moral advance? But we must leave this contradiction unresolved. Other systems with a profoundly moral bearing have also maintained the doctrine of necessity. And it was plainly the intention of the Stoics that the Wise Man, by raising himself to the consciousness of universal necessity, should become free, while all those who had not attained to this consciousness remained in bondage. 'Lead me, Zeus, and thou Destiny,' says Cleanthes, in another fragment, whithersoever I am by you appointed. I will follow not reluctant; but even though I am unwilling through badness, I shall follow none the less.' Yet still with the Stoics the individual element remained equally valid; the individual consciousness was the starting-point of their thought; and hence the difficulty arose, as in modern times, how to reconcile the opposite ideas of individual freedom, and of a world absolutely predetermined by divine reason. To the task of this reconciliation Chrysippus devoted himself, and Cicero describes him as labouring painfully to explain how all things happen by Fate, and yet that there is something in ourselves.' To effect this, he drew a distinction between predisposing and determinant causes, and said that only the predisposing causes rested with Fate, while the 'determinant' cause was always in the human will. This distinction will hardly bear much scrutiny. When Chrysippus was confronted with what philosophers called the lazy argument—namely, the very simple question. Why should I do anything, if all is fated? Why, for instance, should I send for the doctor, since, whether I do so or not, the question of my recovery is already fixed by fate?—to this he replied, It is perhaps as much fated that you should send for the doctor, as that you should get well; these things are confatal.' In other words, the fate of the Stoics was, of course, a rational fate, acting, not supernaturally, but by the whole chain of cause and effect. The reasonings of Chrysippus are interesting historically, as being the first attempt to meet some of the difficulties of the doctrine of human freedom; and much that he urges has been repeated in after times. We have already seen the optimism of Cleanthes expressed in his hymn. He says on the one hand, that nothing is evil in the hands of God; God fits good and evil together into one frame. On the other hand, he says that God does all that is done in the world, except the wickedness.'

Chrysippus, touching on the existence of evil and the afflictions which happen to good men, says that the existence of evil is necessary, as being the contrary to good; without it, good could not exist. Again, that as in a large family a little waste must occur, so in the world there must be parts overlooked and neglected. Again, that the good are afflicted not as a punishment, but 'according to another dispensation.' Again, that evil demons may preside over some parts of the world. Of these inconsistent arguments the first is, perhaps, the most philosophical. It is taken from Heraclitus, according to whom all things exist by the unity of contradiction. Plutarch objects to this argument, that if good can only exist by implying evil, what will become of the good after the conflagration of the world, when Zeus is all in all? If evil is destroyed, then good will be destroyed also; an objection hard to answer from the point of view of Chrysippus.

The Stoics generally professed themselves on the side of the 'common notions.' They accepted the popular theology in an allegorizing spirit, as being a slightly perverted expression of the truth. Though denying the marvellous and the supernatural, and being quite unable to attribute to God a meddling in the minutiae of human affairs, they yet declared for the reality of omens, oracles, and portents. They explained their belief by saying that there was no special revelation, but that certain signs were universally preordained to accompany certain events. The portent and the thing to be signified were 'confatal.' Thus the world was full of divine coincidences, if men could but discern them. We can well fancy that this theme would suit the subtle intellect of Chrysippus, who appears to have written two books on Divination, one on Oracles, and one on Dreams. But a difference on the subject afterwards arose in the school, and Panaetius expressed his doubts as to the reality of divination. With regard to the doctrine of future rewards and punishments, the Stoics were opposed to the general belief. Chrysippus finds fault with Plato for having, in the person of Cephalus, adopted such a vulgar bugbear. But they asserted the moral government of the world, saying that the good alone are happy, and that misfortunes happen to the wicked by Divine Providence. The Stoics would seem excluded by their theological system from holding the immortality of the soul. If all the world by conflagration sinks into the essence of God, how can the individual soul continue to exist? But Cleanthes and Chrysippus spoke of the continuance of the souls of the wise, and the possible continuance of all souls, until the next conflagration.

And, as Zeller says, since the Stoics thus admitted a future existence of limited, but yet indefinite, length—the same practical results followed from their belief as from the current belief in immortality. The statements of Seneca that this life is a prelude to a better; that the body is a lodging-house, from which the soul will return to its own home; his joy in looking forward to the day which will rend the bonds of the body asunder, which he, in common with the early Christians, calls the birthday of eternal life; his description of the peace of the eternity there awaiting us, of the freedom and bliss of the heavenly life, of the light of knowledge which will there be shed on all the secrets of nature; his language on the future recognition and happy society of souls made perfect; his seeing in death a great day of judgment, when sentence will be pronounced on everyone; his making the thought of a future life the great stimulus to moral conduct here; even the way in which he consoles himself for the destruction of his soul by the thought that it will live again in another form hereafter —all contain nothing at variance with the Stoic teaching, however near they may approach to Platonic or even Christian modes of thought. Seneca merely expanded the teaching of his school in one particular direction, in which it harmonizes most closely with Platonism.'

In like manner we see the Roman Cato fortifying his last hours with arguments and ideas drawn not from the orthodox authorities of Stoicism, but from the Phaedo of Plato. It was but natural that in the history of Stoicism a tendency should be evinced to sympathise with Plato in exalting the idea of a future life. If there be any principle in the human mind, short of revelation, which could lead men to trust and believe in their own immortality, it must assuredly be that principle which so largely animated the Stoics, the principle of aspiration, of moral energy, of a life above all ordinary pleasures and interests. And the working of this principle belied and neutralized the logical conclusions of a pantheistic materialism.

The culminating act of self-abnegation with the Stoics was suicide. The first leaders of the school, by their precept and example, recommended the wise, on occasion, to usher themselves out of life. If suicide, thus dignified by a name, were an escape from mere pain or annoyance, it would be an Epicurean act; but as a flight from what is degrading—as a great piece of renunciation, it assumes a Stoical appearance. The passion for suicide reached its height in the writings of Seneca, under the wretched circumstances of the Roman despotism; but, on the whole, it belongs to immature Stoicism—Epictetus and Marcus Aurelius dissuaded from it. In saying this, we cannot for a moment pretend that the Stoical principle ever entirely became clear of alloy; it was too wanting in objective elements—it had too little to draw men out of themselves ever to satisfy the human spirit, ever to be otherwise than very imperfect. Stoical pride will always be a just subject of reproach; for the development of the subjective element of morality necessary to the deepening of the thoughts of the world was overdone by the Stoics, and they supplied nothing in counterbalance. It is not as a complete system, or with any inherent capacity for completeness, certainly not as a rival to Christianity, that we regard the Stoical Idea; but only as a strange and interesting doctrine which has played an important part in the history of the world.

II. The Stoical doctrine was not destined to remain the property of a mere school in Athens; owing to the active intercommunion of nations round the shores of the Mediterranean which took place after the conquests of Alexander, this influence, as well as others, rapidly spread. We have seen how Stoicism owed its origin to the East, and upon the East it apparently reacted at a very early period. This is especially exemplified in the history of the Jews. There seems little doubt that during the third century B.C. many of the Jews became indoctrinated with the teaching of one or other of the two great Greek schools, the Stoic and the Epicurean. The original founder of the sect of the Sadducees was Antigonus of Socho (the master of Zadok), who taught that men should not serve God like hirelings, for a reward. This Antigonus appears to have lived during the former half of the third century, and he is the first Jew who is recorded to have borne a Greek name. It is conjectured that he had travelled in Greek cities, and through admiration for Greek philosophy and culture, adopted a Greek name, and that he had heard Epicurus, or one of his followers, at Athens, and that his subsequent theological teaching became modified by the Epicurean repudiation of future rewards and punishments. However this may be, it is, to say the least, remarkable that the sect of the Pharisees should have arisen about this time, bearing a relation to that of the Sadducees so much analogous to the relation of the Stoics to the Epicureans. Josephus says that the Jews had had for a long time three kinds of philosophy, and that the sect of the Pharisees came very near that of the Stoics. And in describing the Pharisaic doctrines he uses terms that seem borrowed from Stoicism; he says that 'the Pharisees ascribe all things to Fate and God;' that according to them, to act what is right or the contrary lies principally in the power of men, although Fate does cooperate in every action;' that they teach that 'the souls of good men only are removed into other bodies;' and that (Antiq, xviii. i. 3) those who have lived virtuously will have liberty to live again, which seems to be a modification of the Stoical eschatology. It is said by the author lately referred to that the Chasidim, or Assideans of Maccabean times, invested their conservative Judaism to some extent with a Stoic garb and that the Fourth Book of Maccabees exhibits to us Stoicism associated and interwoven with Judaic legalism.' It is the object of the same writer to prove that the Book of Ecclesiastes, to which he assigns a date about 200 B.C., contains references to both Stoical and Epicurean tenets, and was written with the object of dissuading from the study of both these philosophies, which at the time were exerting among the theocratic people an influence adverse to the ancient faith of Judaism. The relation of Stoicism to the Talmud is a question which, if worked out, might probably furnish some interesting results. And of the influence produced by the Stoical modes of thought and phraseology upon the mind of St. Paul, his epistles furnish ample evidence.

St. Paul was born at Tarsus, a meeting point between the East and the West, the congenial soil and chief fatherland of Stoicism. Six of the eminent Stoic teachers had their home there, Chrysippus and Aratus belonged to the neighbouring Soli, and three other leaders of the sect to Mallos, which was also a Cilician town. St. Paul was brought up as a Pharisee, in a sect which had a natural, and probably an historical, affinity with the Stoical doctrines. His master was Gamaliel, the most liberal teacher of the day, who had no dread of Greek learning.' St. Paul's writings show him to have imbibed the current Greek cultivation. When he came to Athens, after encountering certain philosophers of the Epicureans and of the Stoics, he stood up in the midst of Mars' Hill' and addressed the multitude. While speaking to the mass of the Athenians, and making its popular superstition his starting-point, St. Paul appears to appeal to the philosophic part of his audience, weaving in their ideas into his speech, referring to their literature, and producing a studied coincidence with their modes of expression.' Thus the cosmopolitan theory of the Stoics seems distinctly assumed, and both Aratus and Cleanthes may be comprehended under the terms certain of your own poets have said;' and in the saying that 'God dwelleth not in temples made with hands'

St. Paul agrees remarkably with the expressions of Zeno. But it was not merely when he was addressing an Athenian audience that St. Paul made use of Stoical forms of expression. As the speculations of Alexandrian Judaism had elaborated a new and important theological vocabulary, so also to the language of Stoicism, which itself likewise had sprung from the union of the religious sentiment of the East with the philosophical thought of the West, was due an equally remarkable development of moral terms and images. To the Gospel, both the one and the other paid their tribute. As St. John (nor St, John alone) adopted the terms of Alexandrian theosophy as the least inadequate to express the highest doctrines of Christianity, so St. Paul (nor St. Paul alone) found in the ethical language of the Stoics expressions more fit than he could find elsewhere to describe in certain aspects the duties and privileges, the struggles and triumphs, of the Christian life.'

Having now traced some indications of the effect produced by Stoicism on the eastern shores of the Mediterranean, let us turn to watch its promulgation in the West and throughout the Roman world in general, where it was destined to play the part of, to some extent, a regenerating element in the last days of Pagan civilisation. There was a direct succession, as we have seen above, in the lists of the Stoic doctors from Chrysippus to Posidonius, and Posidonius was master to Cicero. During the interval spanned by these successive teachers (from 200 B.C. to 50 B.C.), many circumstances turned the tide of philosophy towards Rome, and commenced the intellectual subjugation of the victors in the domain of thought as well as of imaginative literature. The first awakenings of the national curiosity are somewhat obscured. Aulus Gellius records a decree of the Senate, of the date B.C. 161, for banishing from Borne philosophers and rhetoricians, at the instance of M. Pomponius, the praetor. This fact appears to stand in isolation. Six years later (BC 55), we hear of the famous embassy of the philosophers sent from Athens to Rome to obtain the remission of a fine. Doubt has been thrown on the reality of this event. But independently of the constant oral tradition from Scipio and Laelius down to Cicero, the historical certainty of the embassy is established by a reference which Cicero makes to the writings of Clito-machus, a Carthaginian philosopher who settled at Athens, and was disciple to Carneades immediately after the date assigned to the embassy, and who therefore is an undoubted authority for the facts. However, we may easily believe that the story has been decked out and improved. In some accounts, Carneades the Academic, and Diogenes the Stoic, are mentioned as the envoys; but other accounts, probably for completeness' sake, add Critolaus the Peripatetic. And hence it came to be said that these three represented the three styles of oratory—the florid, the severe, and the moderate. Cicero tells us of a philosophic party at Rome, in compliment to whom these particular ambassadors were sent; while, on the other hand, Cato the Censor viewed with impatience their favourable reception, and urged upon the Senate their speedy dismissal. The most interesting anecdote connected with this embassy is that quoted from the works of Clitomachus,—that A. Albinus, the praetor, said to Carneades in the Capitol, before the Senate, 'Is it true, Carneades, that you think I am no praetor because I am not a wise man, and that this is no city, and that there is no true state in it?' To which Carneades replied, 'I don't think so, but this Stoic does.' This story amusingly represents the confusion in the mind of the Roman praetor, who did not distinguish between the philosophical schools, but was struck by the great paradox he had heard, and was not able to comprehend that inner point of view from which it was said that mighty Rome was no city, and the august praetor had no real office or authority at all.

The anti-philosophical party seem to have continued their exertions at Rome, and under the date 93 B.C. we read of a decree of the censors Domitius Enobarbus and Licinius Crassus against the schools in which a new sort of learning was taught by those who called themselves Latin rhetoricians, and where youths wasted their whole days in sloth. This decree is in fine grand Roman style; it says, 'these things do not please us.' But it was in vain to attempt resisting the influx of Greek philosophy, when the leading and most able men warmly welcomed it. Africanus, C. Laelius, and L. Furius were extremely pleased at the embassy, and always had learned Greeks in their company. A little later than 150 B.C., no one was more instrumental in recommending Stoicism to the Romans than Panaetius of Rhodes, whose instructions in Athens were attended by Laelius and his son-in-law. Fanucius, and also by the conqueror of Carthage. Panaetius accompanied the latter on his famous mission to the courts in Asia Minor and Egypt. He is always spoken of as the friend and companion of Scipio and Laelius. He is recorded to have sent a letter to Q. Tubero, on the endurance of pain. Not only by personal intercourse did Panaetius influence the cultivated Romans, but also still more by his books. These seem to have been of a character eminently fitted for the comprehension of the Romans, being extremely practical, avoiding the harshness and severity of the early Stoics, and being free from the forms of dialectic.'

One peculiarity above all, while it made Panaetius a worse Stoic, made him at the same time a more attractive expositor of philosophy, and was only a fulfilment, after all, of the destiny of Stoicism—namely, his tendency to eclecticism. He constantly had Plato, Aristotle, Xenocrates, Theophrastus, Dicas-archus, in his mouth; he was always speaking of Plato as divine, most wise, most holy, and the Homer of philosophers. We can form a very good conception of his writings from Cicero's work On Offices, which is taken almost exactly from Panaetius' On Things Suitable. An extract verbatim, from the latter, is preserved by Aulus Gellius. It recommends those who are mixed up in affairs to be on their guard, like pugilists, against every sort of attack. It is in rhetorical style, and full of a sensible worldly prudence. Such prudence is no more alien from a particular phase of Stoicism, than it is from a particular phase of religion.

Posidonius (B.C. 135-50) maintained the same intercourse with the Romans, and the same eclectic tendencies as his master. After the death of Panaetius (B.C. 112), he made some extensive travels for the sake of physical inquiry. At Cadiz he spent some time in observations on the sunset; he visited Sicily, Dalmatia, and other countries, and finally settled in Rhodes. Strabo, with a sympathy for his geographical knowledge, called him the most learned philosopher of the day.' In the year 86 B.C. he was sent as ambassador to Rome, and became acquainted with Marias. Pompey visited Posidonius twice in Rhodes; and the story goes that on one of these occasions, Posidonius, having a bad fit of the gout, discoursed from his bed to Pompey on the topic 'that virtue is the only good, and that pain is no evil.' Cicero also studied under him in Rhodes; and finally, coming to Rome in his old age (B.C. 51), he died there a short time afterwards, having had as his hearers C. Velleius, C. Cotta, Q. Lucilius Balbus and probably Brutus. Posidonius wrote a commentary on the Timaeus of Plato, apparently to reconcile it with the Stoical physics. He approximated in some things to Aristotle, and even, it is said, to Pythagoras. On divination, however, he reverted to the old Stoical view, abandoning the scepticism of Panaetius. The ancients make mention of the elegance of his style; and Cicero, while dissenting from his opinions on fate and other subjects, speaks of him at the same time with the greatest respect.

Besides those Stoics who were of eminence and originality enough to advance, though only by amalgamation, the traditional doctrine, there were by this time many others who received it merely and adopted it as an article of faith, without thinking of addition or change. Such was probably Antipater of Tyre, who became the friend and instructor of Cato the younger. And now we find, in the last half-century before Christ, frequent instances of a new fashion in Rome— namely, for a great man to maintain a philosopher in his house, as in modem days a private confessor. Of this custom Cato of Utica was himself an instance, for he is reported to have made a journey to Pergamus with the express object of inducing the famous Stoic Athenodorus, surnamed Cordylion, to accompany him to Rome, in which mission he succeeded, and brought back the sage in triumph, who ended his days in the house of Cato. After this, at Utica, Cato appears to have had among the members of his family Demetrius a Peripatetic, and Apollonides a Stoic. On the night before Cato's suicide, they disputed with each other on the paradox that the Wise Man only is free, Cato warmly supporting the Stoical side.

Another Athenodorus, of the same sect, but surnamed Cananites, was highly honoured by the great Augustus. Attracting the notice of the Emperor at Apollonia, where he held a school, he was invited to Rome, and had the young Claudius placed under his instruction. In his old age returning to Tarsus, he seems to have procured some advantages for his country through his influence with Augustus. Among the few works attributed to him there is one with an eminently Stoical title, On Earnestness and Education.

Arguing by analogy from these external indications, we may imagine the Roman nation at this period imbibing Greek philosophy, or so-called philosophy, at every pore. The Romans, indeed, had not the slightest stomach for metaphysics, and in no one of their writers do we find any trace of a real acquaintance with the systems of Plato or Aristotle. But we can find abundant traces of an acquaintance with Epicurus and Chrysippus and Pansetius and Posidonius. The inducement of the Romans in taking up with this kind of literature was twofold: first, a natural affinity for practical moralising and maxims of life; second, a rhetorical necessity —the desire to turn sentences, to be terse, apposite, and weighty. The constant practice of declamation gave an immense stimulus to the sermonising tendency of the day, and as the despotism of the Empire shut up other subjects, declamation became more and more exclusively moral. Instruction under some Greek rhetorician became part of the education of a Roman youth, and in Athens, Rhodes, Marseilles, and Alexandria, everywhere throughout the great Roman world. Sophists and declaimers might be heard setting forth the theses of the different schools, among which the florid paradoxes of the Stoics were no doubt most striking and attractive.

The Romans who took any side in philosophy invariably became either Epicureans, Stoics, or Academics, or else, as was not unfrequent, they combined the Academical opinions on knowledge with the Stoical morals or some admixture of the Stoical physics. This was the case with L. Lucullus, with M. Brutus, and Terentius Varro. Cicero's creed we know to have been a learned and sensible eclecticism, a qualified Stoicism with a use of the Academic arguments, and an approach in some things to the Peripatetic views. Such a compound was suitable to a statesman and a man of letters; it exhibits acuteness, refinement, breadth of view, and an affinity to what is elevated in the different systems: but at the same time it avoids all extremes, and shuns that unity of principle on which philosophy, properly so called, depends. When such a balance as this was wanting, the Romans joined the opposite ranks of the Stoics or the Epicureans. To either side they had certain elements that inclined them. Their capacity for the physical enjoyment of life, their taste for rural ease and the delights of their beautiful villas, and that healthy realism which we find expressed by Lucretius, all tended to recommend the Epicurean doctrine to the Romans. And added to these predis- predisposing causes was the fact that the first book of philosophy written in the Latin language was the work of one Amafinius, setting forth Epicurism. This treatise, though of no merit according to Cicero, had immense influence, and brought over the multitude to adopt its views. Other works of a similar character followed, and through their popular style took possession of the whole of Italy. Of this phase of feeling hardly any trace remains to us, if we except the splendid poem of Lucretius, and the record of one or two great names among the Roman Epicureans, such as Atticus, the friend of Cicero, Cassius, the murderer of Caesar, L. Torquatus, and C. Velleius. Perhaps its most lasting result was the spread of 'a wisdom,' as Livy calls it, 'which had learned to despise the gods.' Epicurism was transient in Rome, like Sentimentalism in England, because alien to the national characteristics; for on the whole the Romans were far more disposed to energy and sublime virtue, and the conquest of external circumstances, than to easy and harmonious enjoyment. "Without a great intellectual capacity for the apprehension of the universal, there was yet something abstract about their turn of mind; this is shown in their love of law, and in the sternness of the high Roman mood. It has been often said that the old Roman worthies were unconscious Stoics. And now, from Cato to M. Aurelius, we find through the Roman empire an immense diffusion of Stoical principles and of the professors of Stoicism.

III. These professors assumed, it appears, not only distinctive principles, but also certain external marks and badges of their sect. We read in Juvenal of the 'long robe' as synonymous with Stoicism; in Persius we read of their close-cropped hair, and their look of having sat up all night; in Tacitus, of their set countenances and gait expressive of virtue. Like their Jewish counterpart, the Pharisees, they were formal, austere, pretentious, and not unfrequently hypocritical. Under the mask of asceticism, they appear sometimes to have concealed gross licentiousness, and under their sanctimonious face the blackest heart. With bitter indignation does Tacitus record the perfidy of Publius Egnatius Celer, the Stoic philosopher, the client, the instructor, and the false friend of Barea Soranos, whom, with his daughter, he betrayed to Nero, by giving the lying evidence which procured their deaths. Such cases as this, however, are to be regarded like stories of the corruption of priests and monks, and to be judged apart, as giving no sufficient clue to the working of the system. Partly they illustrate the maxim that 'corruption is worst which is the corruption of the best;' partly they show that an elevated and spiritual creed is apt, by the very nobleness of its appearance, to attract unworthy followers. We may also add that, beside the tendencies which might logically be connected with this creed, there was a narrowness in the intensity of Stoicism, and an abstract unreality about its ideas, not favourable to the development of the more human virtues.

Acknowledging these things, we may turn away from this ungracious side of the system, and leave it to the tender mercies of the satirists For even externally, Stoicism, on the whole, presented a better aspect and won a better opinion than this from intelligent observers during the early Roman empire. Nothing can be more significant than the accusation brought against C. Rubellius Plautus by Tigellinus. This Plautus was son of Julia, and great-grandson of Tiberius. Becoming an object of suspicion to Nero, he retired— not from the Roman world, for that was impossible, but from the Court—to Asia, where he lived in the pursuit of the Stoic philosophy. Tigellinus, to stir up Nero's hatred against him, declared, 'That man, though of immense wealth, does not even pretend a wish for enjoyment, but is always bringing forward the examples of the ancient Romans. And he has now joined to these ideas the arrogance of the Stoics—a philosophy which makes men turbulent and restless.' It is easy to see that this accusation was a panegyric. It was followed up by an order sent from Nero that Plautus should be put to death. His friends counselled resistance, but Caaranus and Musonius Rufus, two philosophers who were with him, preached the doctrine of resignation and fortitude; and, armed with their suggestions, he met his death unmoved. This manner of death and life was not confined to Plautus: the reigns of Claudius and Nero exhibit a constellation of noble characters, formed on the model of the younger Cato, and showing the same republican front ard the same practical conception of Stoicism ae he did. Such were Caecina Faetus and his heroic wife Arria, who died at the command of Claudius. Such was S. Barea, already mentioned, and such Thrasea, and his son-in-law Helvidius. Seneca, too, in his death, at all events, most be added to the list—a list of martyrs at a time when all good eminence was sure to attract the stroke. There is something perhaps theatrical and affected about the record of these death-scenes. When we think of Cato arguing on the freedom of the wise man, and then reading the Phaedo through the night, before he stabs himself; when we think of Thrasea pouring out a libation of his own blood to Jupiter the Liberator, and discoursing in his last moments with the Cynic Demetrius on immortality—it seems as if these men had played somewhat studied parts. Such scenes appeal to the rhetorical faculty, rather than to the imagination and the heart. But it is the privilege of certain unhappy periods to be rhetorical. It is the privilege of patriots in miserable days to be excited, strained, unnatural. And hence we can understand how it was that from the

Girondists in France the Roman Stoics obtained such sympathy and admiration.

And now let us take some notice of the character and the thought of Seneca, a man who has been most differently estimated, according to the temperament of his judges, and according as he has been taken at his best or his worst. Probably we may admit almost all the accusations against him, and yet end without judging him too hardly. When just rising into success, Seneca was banished by Claudius, on an obscure charge preferred by Messalina. From Corsica, his place of banishment, he addressed what was called a Consolation to Polybius, the freedman of the Emperor, on the death of his brother. Seneca's object in this Consolation was to effect his own recall, and the means he used were the most fulsome and cringing terms of flattery towards Claudius. His mean adulation quite failed in obtaining his pardon; and he was only recalled, after eight years' exile, through the influence of Agrippina, who made him tutor to her son Domitius, the future emperor Nero. In the museum at Naples one sees frescoes brought from Pompeii, which represent a butterfly acting as charioteer to a dragon. These designs were meant to caricature the relationship of Seneca to his pupil Nero. No doubt he was drawn violently and without the power of resistance through much that was unseemly by his impetuous charge. No doubt he tried, with the help of Burrus, to keep the reins straight. But he was obliged to connive and even assist at things which made people say, with natural surprise, 'This is a strange part for a Stoic to play.' The poor painted butterfly behind the dragon could not choose what part he should play. Other things that have been complained of in Seneca are his violent reaction of spite against Claudius, shown in the satire which he wrote upon his death; his reputed avarice, and the enormous fortune which in a short time he actually amassed under Nero; certain scandalous intrigues, with regard to which there really is not evidence enough to enable us to say whether Seneca was guilty of them or not; and lastly, his possible complicity in the murder of Agrippina. Seneca was no Roman, but a Spaniard, and we can fancy how the milk of his flattery towards Claudius turned sour during his eight years' exile, and how deep resentment settled in his heart. With regard to his accumulating wealth when it was in his power to do, we may perhaps explain it to ourselves, by remembering that many ecclesiastics professing a still more unworldly creed than Stoicism have done the same. With regard to his privity to the death of Agrippina, all that can be said is that Seneca was, towards the end of his career, so thoroughly scolded by Nero, that all power of independent action was taken from him. Physically timid and gentle by nature, Seneca was not born to play a consistent and unyielding part. Considering his hideous position, we may well condone his offences. If we study his writings, and especially his letters, we shall see that he possessed one essentially Stoical characteristic—namely, the intense desire for advance and improvement. The picture of the inner life of Seneca, his efforts after self-discipline, his untiring asceticism, his enthusiasm for all that he esteems holy and of good report —this picture, marred as it is by pedantry, and rhetoric, and vain self-conceit, yet stands out in noble contrast to the swinishness of the Campanian villas, and is in its complex entirety very affecting.

The works of Seneca are over-harshly judged by those who have no taste except for metaphysical philosophy, or who, expecting to find such in Seneca, have been disappointed. But if we approach these writings from a different side, and look at them historically and psychologically as the picture of the times and the man, we find them full of interest. If we can endure being a little cloyed with excess of richness in the style, if we can pardon occasional falsity and frequent exaggeration, we shall discover in them a most fertile genius, and a vein of French wit, so to speak, which is always neat and clever, and often surprising, on the tritest moral subjects. Of all sets of letters that have ever been preserved, there is none that exhibits better and more vividly the different phases of a peculiar idiosyncrasy—of a mind under the dominion of a peculiar kind of thought—than the Epistles of Seneca. Let us take a glance at the more striking features of their contents, and see what sort of a working in the heart was produced by Stoicism under the circumstances of the case. The Epistles of Seneca consist of one hundred and twenty-four letters, written almost continuously in the old age of their author, and all addressed to a person of the name of Lucilius. The first point to be noticed about them is their entire abstraction from all public events of the day, an abstraction very Stoical in itself, and very significant also of the ungenial atmosphere of the political world. Only one allusion is there to Nero, where Seneca takes occasion (Ep. 73) to find fault with the opinion that philosophers are necessarily turbulent and refractory, and despisers of the ruling power.

'On the contrary,' he says, ' none are more grateful to him who affords them security and tranquility of life. They must regard the author of these blessings in the light of a parent.' Like Tityrus, they must say that a god has provided them tranquility, and left their cattle to roam and themselves to play the pipe.' ' The leisure thus granted them is indeed godlike, and raises them to the level of the gods.' In such terms does Seneca appreciate the hours of gilded oppression and treacherous reprieve which were conceded him. Most naturally the topics of his correspondence were not political. His letters were uniformly didactic and moral. In them we see developed the passion for self-improvement and for the cultivation of others. Both by nature and from the influences of Stoicism, Seneca was essentially a schoolmaster; it was evidently the foible of his life to be bringing some one on; he was a pedagogue to himself, and he wanted somebody else whom he might lecture. Of this tendency Lucilius was made the victim. On one occasion he seems to have remonstrated, and to have reminded Seneca that he was forty years of age, and rather old for schooling (Ep. 25). But Seneca will not be deterred. He says it shall not be his fault if his friend does not improve, even though the success be not very brilliant. In every shape and from every side he urges upon him cultivation, and once fairly tells him he cannot remain on the footing of friend unless he cultivates himself and improves (Ep. 35). He hails his good deeds with triumph; rejoices to hear that Lucilius lives on terms of familiarity with his slaves (Ep. 47)— 'are they not? ' he asks, 'men like ourselves, breathing the same air, living and dying like ourselves?'—praises a book he has written, lectures him on the economy of time (Ep. i) ; tells him to be select in his reading (Ep. 2); bids him examine himself to see whether he is progressing in philosophy or in life, since only the latter is valuable (Ep. 16); above all, exhorts him without ceasing to get rid of the fear of death, 'that chain which binds us all' (Ep. 26), though he is half afraid, as in one place he naively confesses (Ep. 30), that Lucilius may come to dread his long-winded letters more even than death itself. However, as a compensation, he promises his friend that these epistles shall insure him a literary immortality, just as the letters of Cicero had made the name of Atticus immortal (Ep. 21).

Such is a specimen of the didactic element in the letters of Seneca; the indications of his own self-discipline and conscious self-culture are equally pregnant and still more characteristic. One sentence of his might be taken as the summary and expression of his entire spirit. In speaking of the state of the 'advancing man' as distinguished in Stoical parlance from the 'wise man,' he says (Ep. 71), 'It is a great part of advance to will to be advancing. Of this I am conscious to myself; I will to advance, nay, I will it with my whole heart.'

In the will thus fixed and bent there is often a sort of unreal triumph, independent of actual success or failure. Seneca does not conceal from us his failures in realising his conception of philosophic behaviour. But while he confesses, he is never humbled. Rather he seems proud of detecting his own falling off. On one occasion (Ep. 87) he relates an excursion which he made into the country with a friend, and in which he says they spent 'two delightful days.' They took very few slaves, and one rustic vehicle. On meeting with persons riding in grander equipages, he tells us, he could not refrain from blushing, and secretly wished that they should not think that this sordid conveyance belonged to him.

'I have made but little progress as yet,' he sighs, 'I dare not yet openly assume frugality. I mind the opinions of passers-by.' Whereupon he proceeds to lecture down this weakness in the grandest terms, and occupies many pages of a letter in proving that riches are not a good. On another occasion he recounts a voyage which he had undertaken from Naples to Puteoli (Ep. 53). In these few miles the sea became rough, and the philosopher grew sick, and, unable to endure the horrible sufferings of his position, he commanded the pilot to set him ashore.

'As soon as I had recovered my stomach,' he says, 'I began to reflect what a forgetfulness of our defects follows us about.' Pursuing this train of reasoning, he enters upon the praises of philosophy, and soaring far above sea-sickness, he exclaims, 'Philosophy sets one above all men, and not far behind the gods. Indeed, in one point the wise man might be said even to surpass the Deity; for the Deity is fearless by the gift of nature, but the wise man by his own merits.'

This last saying, which is often quoted against Seneca, is perhaps the most foolish thing he ever said, and must not be taken as an average specimen of his thoughts. One failure which he ascribes to himself may be justly reckoned as a merit; for while dissuading Lucilius (Ep. 63) from overmuch grieving at the loss of a friend, he says, 'I myself so immoderately wept for Annaeus Serenus, that I must rank among the bad examples of those who have been overcome by grief.'

And he reflects that the reason of this weakness must have been that he had not sufficiently considered the possibility of his friend dying first. We may also attribute it to the existence in Seneca of an affectionate heart, which had not been entirely supplanted by the abstractions of Stoicism, not entirely 'sicklied o'er by the pale cast of thought.' After alluding to cases where Seneca confessed to have fallen from the philosophic height, it is surely fair not to leave unrecorded an occasion where he effected an important triumph of the will. The kind of self-discipline chosen was somewhat surprising; it is related in the Fifty-sixth Epistle, where Seneca tells his friend that he had taken lodgings 'over a bath.' He details with minuteness the various mixed and deafening sounds by which his ears were perpetually assailed. He could hear distinctly the strong fellows taking their exercise—throwing out their hands loaded with the dumb-bells —straining and groaning—hissing and wheezing—breathing in every kind of unnatural way—at another moment some one having his shoulders slapped by the shampooer—a hue and cry after a thief—a man practising his voice in the bath—people leaping and splashing down into the water— the various cries of the pie men and sellers of baked meats, as they vended their wares—and several other sounds, to all of which Seneca compelled his mind to be inattentive, being concentrated on itself. The power of abstraction gained by such a discipline he seems to have thought very valuable. At the end of his letter, he declares that as the experiment is quite successful, and as the sounds are really abominable, he has now determined to change his quarters.

About such moral peddling as this there is of course nothing great. But the spirit which actuates it is in its origin deep and good, and is only not admirable when it becomes perverted. The conscious desire for moral progress becomes unfortunately very easily perverted; it degenerates too often into small self-analysis, and that weak trifling which is most utterly opposed to real progression. We find Seneca remaining in his moral nature a strange mixture of the pedant and the schoolboy; on the one hand always teaching himself, and on the other hand with everything to learn; and yet still, with all its imperfections, we may question whether this attitude is not more human and better than anything like an Epicurean acquiescence and content in one's nature as it is. That self-reflection, that communing of man with his own heart, which the tendencies of Stoicism and the course of the world's history had now made common, produced in Seneca occasionally intuitions into the state of the human race, which he expresses in language curious to meet with in the writings of a Pagan. He says:

'Conceive in this vast city, where without cease a crowd pours through the broadest streets, and like a river dashes against anything that impedes its rapid course—this city, that consumes the grain of all lands—what a solitude and desolation there would be if nothing were left save what a severe judge could absolve of fault! We have all sinned (peccammus omnes), some more gravely, others more lightly, some from purpose, others by chance impulse, or else carried away by wickedness external to them; others of us have wanted fortitude to stand by our resolutions, and have lost our innocence unwillingly and not without a struggle. Not only we have erred, but to the end of time we shall continue to err. Even if anyone has already so well purified his mind that nothing can shake or decoy him any more, it is through sinning that he has arrived at this state of innocence.'

Those who have been anxious to obtain the authority of Aristotle for the doctrine of 'human corruption' will find on consideration that this idea, which was historically impossible for a Greek of the fourth century B.C., came with sufficient vividness into the consciousness of persons in the position of Seneca, but not till much later than Aristotle, probably not before the beginning of our era. On the other hand, we are not to fancy that the thoughts of Seneca received any influence from Christianity. We learn from passages like that above quoted, not that Seneca had any acquaintance with Christian doctrines, but that some of the thoughts and feelings which St.

Paul had about the world were had also by Pagans contemporaneous with him.

There is one more characteristic of the letters of Seneca which ought not to be left unmentioned, and that is, the way in which they are perpetually overshadowed by the thought of death. The form assumed by this meditatio mortis is a constant urging of arguments against fearing to die. These arguments are, as might be expected, infinitely varied and ingenious. 'Death,' he says, 'lurks under the name of life. It begins with our infancy.' 'It is a great mistake to look forward to death, since a great part of it is already over. We die daily.' 'Death is no punishment, but the law of nature.' 'Children and idiots do not fear death, why cannot reason attain to that security which folly has achieved?' 'Death is the one port in a stormy sea—it is either end or transition—it brings us back to where we were before birth—it must be a gain or nothing.' 'The apparatus of death is all a cheat; if we tear off the mask, there is nothing fearful.'

'Behind fire and steel and the ferocious crowd of executioners there is death hiding—merely death, which my slave or my waiting-maid has just despised' (Ep. 24). Not content with bringing forward these considerations dissuasive of terror, Seneca in other places does all he can to familiarise the mind with the idea of suicide. He says, 'There is nothing more contemptible than to wish for death. Why wish for that which is in your power?—die at once, if you wish to do so' (Ep. 117). He relates with approbation the suicide of his friend Marcellinue, who, being oppressed with a long and troublesome invalidism, was recommended by a Stoic to give up the trivial round of life; whereupon, having distributed his goods among his weeping slaves, he effected death by a three-days' abstinence from food, betaking himself to a hot bath when his body was exhausted, wherein he fainted and died (Ep. 77). Other instances of self-destruction are scattered through the letters of Seneca, some of which give a sad illustration of the unhappiness of the times. It seems to have been not uncommon for the wretched captives who were doomed to the conflicts of the arena to steal themselves away, sometimes by the most revolting modes of death. And it is surely a miserable sign when cultivated men of the day look on such deeds with pleasure and admiration. So great was the tendency to suicide under Claudius and Nero, that even Seneca on one occasion acknowledges that it is excessive. He says, 'We ought not to hate life any more than death, we ought not to sink into that mere life-weariness to which many are prone who see nothing before them but an unvarying routine of waking and sleeping, hungering and eating.' But the majority of Seneca's arguments are in the other direction. They are the results of a deep sense of unhappiness and insecurity, which existed side by side with his philosophic self-complacency.

They were connected, on the one hand, with a timidity of nature and a real love of life; on the other hand, with a presentiment of evil and a sense of the necessity of preparing for the worst. When death suddenly and actually came upon Seneca—like Cicero, he met it with fortitude, in spite of his timidity, and probably not on account of his previous reasonings, but from an innate elevation of mind called out on emergency. We have observed that Seneca spoke of death as 'either end or transition;' this sums up his views of the future under an alternative. But his real tendency was to Platonic visions of the soul freed from the trammels of the body and restored to freedom. He is unwilling that Lucilius should arouse him from the 'pleasant dream' of immortality. He likes to expatiate on the tranquillity of mind and absolute liberty which await us ' when we shall have got away from these dregs of existence into the sublime condition on high.'

It is a great contrast if we turn from Seneca to Epictetus. It is going from the florid to the severe, from varied feeling to the impersonal simplicity of the teacher, often from idle rhetoric to devout earnestness. No writings of Epictetus remain, but only (what is perhaps equally interesting for us) records of his didactic conversations, preserved as near as possible in his own words by Arrian, the historian, who studied under him at Nicopolis. Epictetus was a lame slave, the property of Epaphroditus, who was himself the freedman and the favourite of Nero. While yet a slave, Epictetus was won over to the Stoic doctrine by Musonius Rufus. Obtaining his freedom, he taught in Rome, and afterwards, when the philosophers were banished from the city by Domitian, in Nicopolis of Epirus. What is most striking about his discourses is their extremely religious spirit, and the gentle purity of the doctrines they advocate. In them Stoicism reached its culmination, and attained an almost entirely un-pagan character; its harsher traits were abandoned, and while Epictetus draws the picture of the wise man under the name of Cynic, there is hardly a trace of anything cynical in the life which he recommends. To mention the subjects of some of his discourses may serve to give an idea of their nature. The following headings strike the eye:

On things in our power and not in our power. How to preserve one's own character in everything. How to follow out the conception that God is Father of mankind. On moral advance. On Providence. On equanimity. How to do all things pleasing to the gods. What part of a sin is one's own. On moral training.

As might be conjectured, there is nothing speculative in these discourses. Epictetus both received and imparted philosophy as a fulfilling of the needs of the soul, not as a mere development of the intellect. His words on this and other subjects present very often a strange coincidence with the language of the Gospel. He says, 'The beginning of philosophy is the consciousness of one's own weakness and inability with regard to what is needful.' 'The school of the philosopher is a physician's house; you should not go out from it pleased, but in pain. For you come not whole, but sick—one diseased in his shoulder and another in his head.' 'Young man, having once heard these words, go away, and say to yourself," Epictetus has not spoken them to me (from whence came they to him ?), but some kind god by his means. It would not have come into the mind of Epictetus to say these things, since he is not accustomed to reason with anyone. Come, then, let us obey God, lest we should move God to anger."' 'The true Cynic should recollect that he is sent as a messenger from Zeus to men, to declare to them concerning things good and evil, and to show them that they seek good where it is not to be found, and where it is to be found they do not desire it.'

With regard to the manifestations of Providence, Epictetus says (Dissert, i. 16, 19): 'What, then; since ye are all blind, is there not need of one who should fill up this place, and sing in behalf of you all the hymn to God? Of what else am I capable, who am a lame old man, except to sing the praises of God? Were I a nightingale, I would do as the nightingale; were I a swan, I would do as the swan. But now, since I have reason, I must sing of God. This is my office, and I perform it, nor will I leave my post, as for as in me lies, and I exhort you to join in the same song.'

'If anyone will properly feel this truth, that we are all especially born of God, and that God is the father of men and gods, I think that such a one will henceforth allow no mean or unworthy thoughts about himself. If Caesar were to adopt you, would not your pride be unbearable; and now that you are the son of Zeus, will you not be elated?'

Such sayings as these are a specimen of the vein of piety which runs through the teachings of Epictetus. In moral life, he exhorts to purity, equanimity, and forgiveness of injuries. He draws a broad line of distinction between things in our power and things out of our power. Within our power are the will and our opinion of things; beyond our power, the body, possessions, authority, and fame. The will itself nothing can touch; bonds, imprisonment, and death itself, do not impair the internal freedom of the will. Lameness impedes the leg, but not the will. True wisdom and happiness consist in placing all one's thoughts and hopes on things within our power—that is to say, on the will itself and the internal consciousness. This attitude will render happiness impregnable, for the wise man will enter no contest save where he is sure of the victory.

In an exaltation of the will, and in thus withdrawing into its precincts, the Stoicism of Epictetus declares itself. To some extent he provided an objective side for his thought, by the pious and theological reflections which he introduced into his philosophy. But they were not sufficiently made to pervade his whole system, and with regard to the question of immortality he contented himself, as far as we know, with certain brief remarks, implying the utter resolution of personality after death. 'Come,' he says, 'but whither?—to nothing dreadful, but only to what is near and dear to thee, to the elements whence thou hast sprung'

The same spirit as that of Epictetus the slave expresses itself in Marcus Aurelius the emperor, whose thoughts have come down to us in the shape of a monologue in twelve books. These last two great Stoical writers appear both to have been influenced by Neo-Platonic views, for which Stoicism, on its spiritual side, had a considerable affinity. The weakness of humanity is a leading idea with Aurelius.

'Of human life,' he says (ii. 17), 'the duration is a point; the substance is fleeting; the perception is dim; the fabric of the body is corruptible, the soul is an idle whirling; fortune is inscrutable, and fame beyond our judgment. In short, all that there is of the body is a stream, and all that there is of the soul is a dream and a smoke. Life is a war, and a lodging in a strange country; the name that we leave behind us is forgetfulness. What is there, then, that can conduct us ? Philosophy alone. . . . Oh, my soul! wilt thou ever be good, and simple, and one, and naked, and more transparent than the body which clothes thee? Wilt thou ever be fall and without a want, desiring nothing, hankering after nothing, whether animate or inanimate, for the enjoyment of pleasure, but content with thy present condition?' (x. i.)

Such are the mystical ecstasies into which Antoninus rises in communing with himself. With these, honest self-examinations and humility of feeling are often combined, and the whole is tempered by a cold spirit of Stoical resignation. Of the philosophy of the Emperor we need not add anything further beyond one slight point—namely, that we find in him the same psychological division of man into body, soul, and spirit, as had also been employed by St. Paul. We may take our leave of the monologue of Antoninus by quoting from it his feeling about the Christian martyrs. 'The soul,' he says, 'when it must depart from the body, should be ready to be extinguished, to be dispersed, or to subsist a while longer with the body. But this readiness must proceed from its own judgment, and not from mere obstinacy, as with the Christians; it must be arrived at with reflection and dignity, so that you could even convince another without declamation.'

In Marcus Aurelius we appear at first sight to have the desire of Plato fulfilled. We see a philosopher on the throne. But even absolute power does not give influence or sway. Plato wished the whole State to bend and turn under the control of omnipotent wisdom, as the limbs of a man would follow the impulses of his mind. But very far was Marcus Aurelius from being gifted with that sort of electric force which could put itself out and transform the world, even if the Roman empire were not too huge and too corrupt for such a process. Philosophy in general must be considered as something incapable of coming immediately into contact with politics and practical life, and the philosophy of Antoninus consisted peculiarly in a withdrawal from the world, in self-examination, moral progress, and thoughts about God.

While the Emperor was thus busied more with his own soul than with penetrating State reforms, the world enjoyed a halcyon time. The ruler was mild, just, and forgiving; he had only one deficiency, but that the greatest which could possibly attach to him, namely, an utter want of insight into character. The sole exception to his clemency was that, excited probably by the narrow malignance of his fellow Stoics—he condescended to persecute the Christians. The adoration of the people showed how much the gentleness of Marcus Aurelius was appreciated—but it is not the mild monarchs who leave permanent blessings to their country. Among his most public tastes seems to have been a fondness for jurisprudence; he produced several volumes of Constitutions. This province of industry was the one most attractive of the day. In the absence of literature, Roman jurisprudence is the one great and lasting product of the age of the Antonines. And now a word must be said upon an often mooted and never thoroughly discussed subject—the influence of the Stoic philosophy upon Roman law. Acquaintance with Grecian philosophy in general began at Rome contemporaneously with a change in the laws. The first epoch of Roman law was an epoch of rigid forms, and a narrow but coherent system, exclusively adapted to Roman citizens. Commerce and conquest made it necessary that law should widen so as to embrace the inhabitants of the Italian States. Hence the growth of the praetor's adjudicating power. By degrees the decisions of the praetors in regard to the hitherto over-exclusive laws of property, and the rights of persons born out of the Roman city, grew up into a body of equity by the side of the civil law. This body of equity, which was framed on the principles of natural reason, of course reflected the highest general enlightenment and the most cultivated ideas of the jurisconsults of the day. We have already seen that during the first and second centuries B.C. the most eminent Romans attached themselves to the direct study of Greek philosophy. To the list of the disciples of the Stoics we may add some names more immediately connected with jurisprudence. C. Aquilius Gallus and Lucilius Balbus, distinguished jurisconsults of the time of Cicero, studied again under Scaevola; and Balbus, who in Cicero's Be Nature Deorum is made the expositor of the Stoical view, was teacher of Servius Sulpicius. Equity attained in the eyes of such persons an immense preference over the civil law. To this tendency of opinions Cicero gave a great stimulus, maintaining, as he did always, that justice must be based on humanity and reason, and that the source and rule of right were not to be sought in the laws of the Twelve Tables, but in the depths of the human 'intelligence.' Now, if we wish to form an idea to ourselves of the sort of way in which philosophy at Rome influenced jurisprudence, we may think of the philosophy of Cicero, that is, a philosophy not exclusively Stoical, but eclectic, practical, and human. Even the philosophers of the Stoic school themselves were by this time, as we have seen, all eclectic. Much more, then, would the lawyers avoid any rigid adherence to one set of formulas; they would be sure to accept a certain mixture and modification of views. A number of humane and enlightened principles were now diffused, and it is perhaps true that the most noble of these ideas were due primarily to Stoicism—as, for instance, the cosmopolitan thought, that the world is our State, and that mankind are of one race, being all the children of God. But it is true also that the general course of history had tended to foster and develop this and other ideas which Stoicism forcibly enunciated.

In the growth, then, of the Roman 'Jus Gentium,' and in the amelioration and softening of many austere legal usages (as, for instance, the absolute authority of fathers over their children), we see not simply and solely the influence of Stoicism, but of a generally enlightened practical philosophy, in which Stoicism was not more than an important element. But besides the material alterations which occurred in the spirit of the Roman laws, besides the era of the Jus Praetorium, we must look in another direction—to the era of 'codification,' if we wish to trace philosophical influences. An eminent authority maintains that the Stoical philosophy was to Roman jurisprudence what Benthamism has been to English law'—namely, a directing influence that came into play in the absence of any absolutely determining causes. These two principles of action might be said to be diametrically opposite to each other; for Benthamism, which looks to utility, commences with the concrete; while it is the essence of Stoicism to take an abstract point of view. The writings of Zeno and Chrysippus on the 'universal state' are lost, so we know not its details as conceived by them, but we may be sure that if Stoicism had had the framing of the laws for the Roman empire entrusted to its hands, there would have been a logical deduction from the principle of the natural freedom and equality of the whole human race. But what do we find? That slavery, even under Justinian, was mitigated, and not abolished; that men of different ranks were not equal in the sight of the law; that the civil incapacity of women (which Zeno had denied) still remained; that the application of cruel punishments, and even of torture, was treated by the new codes in a way which showed more a respect for existing usage and for the old statutes than a disposition to legislate synthetically from philosophical principles. Gaius, Papinian, and Paulus, appear very timid by the side of Seneca and Epictetus. Perhaps this belongs of necessity to the progress of jurisprudence, that it must not break too hastily with the past: but we are obliged, if this view be correct, to confine the influence of Stoicism on Roman law to the introduction of an idea of form, to the endeavour to bring the actual under the scope of certain abstract formulae. We must not expect to find the logical and systematic development of these formulae, but rather we must recognise a frequent antithesis between abstract principles and the details to which one might have expected them to be applied. And yet again it appears, if we look a little further, that the philosophical ideas to which the Jurists appealed, though not immediately triumphant over all other considerations in the Roman Code, did yet in some cases come into direct application; and what is of far more importance, that these principles, being enunciated with reverence, were held up for the admiration of posterity, and so came to exert an influence on the whole bearing of subsequent jurisprudence. When we read in the Digest the stately preamble concerning the Jus Naturale—which nature has taught all animals, and which is prior even to the Jus Gentium prevailing among the human race—we are apt to be most struck with the abstract and, we might almost say, futile appearance of such a principle, followed out afterwards with so little consistency. But the idea of the 'Law of Nature,' enunciated here and elsewhere in the Roman Code, being taken up by Grotius and the Continental Jurists, became a leading idea of jurisprudence, the characteristic principle of a particular school, and the antithesis of Benthamism. What is the meaning of this conception, the 'Law of Nature,' and whether it has any reality or value as separate from, or opposed to, utility and experience, is a matter of keen debate amongst philosophical Jurists. It is not the province of the present Essay to enter upon this question. That which is our concern we may dismiss with only two remarks of recapitulation: First, the idea of the Law of Nature, as introduced into the Roman law, was not by any means purely Stoical, but was the result of the general growth of ideas in the first century B.C., and was vividly apprehended by the eclectic and practical Cicero; second, this idea, though subsequently so influential, was not by any means uniformly applied in the details of the Corpus Juris.

Whatever fragments of Stoicism were preserved in the Roman law descended, no doubt, as a contribution not only to modem law, but also to modern morals. In other channels the direct connection of our own thoughts with the ancient Stoics is hard to trace, because, long before modem thought began a separate existence, Stoicism had sunk into the world, and had influenced the ideas of men far beyond its own immediate school. But in acknowledging the influence of ancient civilisation at all, in acknowledging the impress of Cicero and Tacitus, and even of the Fathers of the Church, we acknowledge to an appreciable extent a debt to Stoicism. This, while arising in a form of a Greek philosophy, was at the same time a reaction, from a Semitic point of view, against the Grecian and the philosophical spirit. Hence its affinity to modern feelings. We have seen how it held up the delights of an inner life as preferable to all tangible and palpable enjoyments, however innocent they might be; we have seen how it drew the mind away from external realities into an abstract ideal; how it delighted in the conception of moral progress and the triumph of will; how it developed the thought of duty and the responsibility of the individual; how, deserting the restrictions of national politics, it raised itself to conceive of all mankind as one brotherhood, each member standing in direct relation to God; finally, we have seen how, following its natural tendencies. Stoicism became more and more exclusively theological in its views. To some extent, then, this doctrine supplied the needs of the human soul and the wants of a spiritual religion. Running parallel with Christianity, and quite uninfluenced by it, it yet exhibited the development of pure, gentle, and unworldly thoughts in the mind. It showed us how high it was possible for the Pagans to reach. At the same time it bore upon its face its own imperfection, its one-sidedness, and its unnatural and paradoxical character.

Made in United States
Orlando, FL
21 December 2021

12253658R00067